Au lecteur   (To The Reader

It seems to always come down to this. I do not know where things are going.

... عن طريق Arabic, (Tariq) a path, a way... ... of a new book of my works, I ask: 'Who did this?'

At the beginning of his own book, Nadja, André Breton asks, "Who am I?"

.... led me to la poésie, to poetry, to the path of being a poet...wandering in this world. My (American) mentor, Walt Whitman: Song Of The Open Road, Leaves Of Grass, that became my bible (age 18(?)) Schubert's music, Der Wanderer ... My compières French Surrealists ... Ethiopic ancestors who accompanied the Queen Of Sheba, her singers sing on in my blood: Armenian troubadors — Ashoughs! Arabic poets ...(fedele of Ibn 'Al Arabi)

Of course — bien sur — I owe so much to France — for language la langue Woman all the more beautiful in eschewing furs and leather! To Alexandre Dumas — a person métisse — of mixed African race like myself ... And to the beauty and courage of Woman! — who inspires (yes, I use that word!) me on my journey toward the Marvellous, Le Merveilleux.

"We are Life's Guests!" words of (yet another mentor) Boris Pasternak (poet, Author of Dr. Zhivago)

À Vous,
♡ Sotère أُلشَّاعر

On the Planet without Visa

Selected Poetry and Other Writings,
AD 1960–2012

Sotère Torregian

COFFEE HOUSE PRESS
MINNEAPOLIS
2012

Coffee House Press books are available to the trade through our primary distributor, Consortium Book Sales & Distribution, cbsd.com. For personal orders, catalogs, or other information, write to: Coffee House Press, 79 Thirteenth Avenue NE, Suite 110, Minneapolis, MN 55413.

Coffee House Press is a nonprofit literary publishing house. Support from private foundations, corporate giving programs, government programs, and generous individuals helps make the publication of our books possible. We gratefully acknowledge their support in detail in the back of this book.

Good books are brewing at coffeehousepress.org

LIBRARY OF CONGRESS CATALOGING-IN-PUBLICATION DATA
Torregian, Sotère.
On the planet without visa : selected poetry and other writings,
1960–AD2012 / Sotère Torregian.
P. CM.
ISBN 978-1-56689-301-5 (ALK. PAPER)
I. Title.
PS3570.069305 2012
811'.54—DC22
2011029281
PRINTED IN THE UNITED STATES
1 3 5 7 9 8 6 4 2
FIRST EDITION | FIRST PRINTING

ACKNOWLEDGEMENTS:
"The Newark Public Library Reading Room" first appeared in *New Black Voices: An Anthology of Contemporary Afro-American Literature,* ed. Abraham Chapman, originally published by Signet, 1972.

"From Russian Hill" has appeared in the *Paris Review* and in *The Age of Gold*, originally published by the Kulcher Foundation, 1976.

Interview "In a Coffee House and in a Car: An Interview with Sotère Torregian," conducted by Becky Morgan for *The World* magazine's "World Interview Issue," edited by Anne Waldman. Originally published by The Poetry Project at St. Mark's Church, in 1974.

"With Lita Hornick and 'Bear' at Trader Vic's, New York" from *Amtrak Trek: Being Poems and Prose Written Cross-Country from California to New York*, originally published by Telephone Books, 1979.

"On Another Weekend of *The Thin Man*" first appeared in *"I Must Go" (She Said) "Because My Pizza's Cold": The Selected Works, 1957–1999*, originally published by Skanky Possum Press in 2002.

The poems "From the Broadside, 'Addenda (For August 15th'" were originally published in a broadside by Sylvestre Pollet of Backwoods Broadsides.

"Prolegomena" first appeared in *Kadar Koli*, published by Habenicht Press.

"On Brubeck Way" originally appeared in *The Pacifican*.

ON THE PLANET WITHOUT VISA

Works, 1960–1970

Works, 1970-1990

Works, 1990 - 2000

Works, 2000 — 2012

Editor's Note

When we first read Sotère Torregian's poems, and admittedly, without knowing enough about the poet himself, we believed that Torregian, or S. T., as he often refers to himself, was a very skilled but non-native speaker of English. The French-style punctuation, the occasional spellings that derive from British English, and the subject matter combined to read as if he were a native of the Mediterranean. However, in his long-form essay "Où la Vrai Vie, or, the 'Real' Surreal Life" Torregian explains that he claims French "not by nationality but by vision." We were surprised to find out that while Sotère Torregian makes his intellectual and aesthetic home in the Mediterranean he's never been there in person or in fact outside of the United States.

Torregian actively curates his world—a space from which he can explore questions of identity, citizenship, race, and belonging—with a rich imagination, curiosity, and, above all, a deep sense of humanism. He has an unending facility for finding inspiration in the quotidian, taking it from Greek tragedy and *Sesame Street* alike. He has taught himself multiple languages, reads voraciously, and corresponds tirelessly with friends. Throughout his seventy years, Torregian has created his own nationality, adopting first the identity of the cosmopolitan and finally that of a poet of the French Surrealist persuasion.

Torregian does not write his works using a computer; he has access to one only when he goes to the public library or visits family. He works from memory, without the benefit of the electronic resources and tools—on-line dictionaries, Wikipedia, or spell check—on which most of us rely.

It follows that you will see imperfect references in these poems, perhaps the title of a collection of poems, a symphony, or a play slightly askew. These imperfections are part of the point, part of the slippery persona of the poet. Torregian never falters when it comes to representing what the essence of the work means to him or how the work in question contributes to the construction of his identity. As you will see in each poem and essay, creating an entire world for yourself takes constant feeding, maintenance, and inspiration. The editing we have done in conjunction with the author has largely been for the purpose of preserving the consistency of Sotère's vision and the timbre of his voice. In his poem "Hurry My Verses, Hurry!" Torregian writes "Let these / lines go forth as emissaries." We hope they do just that.

Sotère Torregian, Literally

The pleasures of Sotère Torregian's poetry—in its good-news aspect, so to speak—derive in part from the sensation of the poems' hurtling onward, each one through a space, light or dark, of its own making. On the page, the lines are clear and succinct, with a musicality indistinct from the turns of intimated sense. Most take shape as declarative sentences bearing, as they will, the aura—and authority—of plain fact. A poem from 1967 begins briskly enough: "Today I ate a donut"; another, nearly forty years later, says "There are Greek armies under the sink." (Which is more fanciful, Greek armies or a donut, is up for grabs.) As such statements accumulate, the poem they add up to achieves momentous life: "Each day is a day of ingenuity," Torregian writes, so every poem finds its own peculiar urgency.

Fearless this poetry seems, and no less assertive of a deep respect for both its manifold sources and a destination imagined as it goes along. (Torregian would probably approve of Paul Valéry's remark that a poem is written by someone other than the poet and addressed to someone other than the reader.) The aforementioned headlong quality probably has to do with "French Surrealism," a term for what Torregian early on found most congenial among the strains of modern European visual art and poetry, but one that occurs within his own work as a kind of ongoing lyric conceit. The conceit is thematic, part of Torregian's world view. Like Arshile Gorky—with whom he shares a history of personal displacement countered by radical self-invention, as well as a brief but helpful brush with Surrealism in its official guise—his surreal moments feel instinctive rather than programmatic. There are no unearned ambiguities, no absolutes without some direct perceptual base. (The title of one of Gorky's paintings *The Leaf of the Artichoke Is an Owl* is fair match for the sort of perceptual surreal Torregian has practiced throughout his career.) Torregian doesn't seek out mystery, he just encounters it in his experiences as they come, as he articulates them. Likewise, if Surrealism gave us the possibility of the twentieth-century love poem as a form of rhetorical liftoff, Torregian has naturalized it as an everyday eventuality: *Forget that there is history / and hold me.*

The more off-guard Torregian finds the world (and in it, himself), the greater amplitude available for saying what is there. Also, due to circumstances literally beyond his control, there are perforce several languages with which the saying takes place; the result is a vocabulary renewed and charged regularly, like Walt Whitman's, by fresh additions—and also in Torregian's case, the attraction of second-language oddities ("arquebuses" and "transmitotic," for two) and the exquisitely formal or slightly archaic ("bald pate") placed bull's-eye fashion in proper context. As a quadraphone (and then some), Torregian has this lingual distinction that allows his poetry to act as a kind of cradle of civilized discourse, and further, to effect a type of contemporary high literary style in an age when such heights are rarely even attempted.

Ultimately, Torregian's ideas and feelings—including those about poetry and its efficacy—are all his own, and inextricable from the words in which he has located them. In this, he is, as Willem de Kooning said of Marcel Duchamp, a one-man movement. His multiple alliances with such literary groupings as the New York School and the Négritude of Leopold Senghor and Aimé Césaire—along with his fellow feeling for New Jersey confreres so haphazardly arrayed as Amiri Baraka, Allen Ginsberg, David Shapiro, and Joseph Ceravolo—are first of all autobiographical markers, although readily transmuted by Torregian himself into continuous reaffirmations of a one-of-a-kind (though also kindred across boundaries) poetic faith. It is this faith that remains so astonishing; reading the poems, one is struck by both the consistency and the palpable lightness with which he declares it. (He never fails to credit, as an instance of advice continually taken to heart, Ted Berrigan's long-ago street-corner admonition "Lighten up!"—against the drag of the then-beginner's self-seriousness.) Concomitantly, for the duration of encountering the work with all its quick shifts and other imaginative excitations (have I mentioned the sheer knowing cheerfulness that pervades this book?), the reader gets to share in such belief and splendor:

* As I was saying the great disadvantage of the modern
  man's dress shirt is that it's without a pocket
  thence when you go to grasp for a pen there's
  nothing there but air! Geronimo
  never had to worry about that, except in
  his last days when he signed autographs for fans while
  motoring about in his Model T Inexplicable sister
  of the Minotaur enigma and masque As you're just in from Dakar
  To catch you in an embrace as you drop
  your trench coat It was a "last-minute" decision
  to expend the lines of the poem to go off
  the page just this once

The poems are nothing if not sincere.

—Bill Berkson

* From the poem "Pancakes and Champagne for Breakfast"

Note from the Author

—Wahoo! This is AD 2012! Most of us who grew up in the 1940s and/or 1950s never thought we'd see year *AD 2000.* It was, after all, "Buck Rogers's era," "Buck Rogers in the Twenty-First Century," et al., a mythological time,—but very real to those of us who viewed the Saturday matinees at the movies or the serials on early (circa 1951) American TV, stratocruisers and ray guns and interplanetary adventures of the Buck Rogers clan. So, we're *in it* now, the once-fabled "Twenty-First Century" *minus* Buck (Buster Crabbe) but with a bevy, though, of really nasty scary characters and creatures on the national and international scenes; and, strangely enough, strangely enough, *poetry* has *survived!* And poets, too! Anne Waldman, Eleni Sikelianos, and John Ashbery, too, are still "here". Yet many have left for the Happy Hunting Ground of the Sky Father: Ted (Berrigan), "Uncle" Kenneth (Koch), the inimitable Frank (O'Hara); and Joe (Ceravolo). one of my closest friends. These were all and remain friends of the New York days and beyond . . ..

My eternal gratitude for their friendship and supportiveness through years of indecision and crisis as well as self-questioning. Thanks to Lita Hornick and *KULCHUR Press.*

But this is not an *Apologia Pro Vita Sua*

It's simply an improvised *Hello,* or *Je Reviens,* or *Bonjour!*

As for my French Surrealist compères, only Nanos Valoritis lives on in California. (Who can survive in Paris these days without the inheritance bequeathed by a billionaire grandfather? One could, however, survive, in the days of the *bateau lavoire* of Max Jacob and Apollinaire in the Monmartre of 1913. Paris: some inexpensive red wine, frommage, baguettes, select vegetables in season off the stands at *Les Halles,* a compassionate wealthy mistress such as was (Picasso's) Fernande Olivier . . .)

But I'm *here,* not there. (Where*ever* "there" is)

Exile can be fruitful (*l'Amerique Exil perpetuel*)

It is my shadow (*mon ombre*) that lives here in California and my real *selbst* in Paris or vice versa?

If it *is* my shadow that's living here, then it has an appetite and a sex drive still for beautiful women and it still has the need to write poems and/or *écritures automatiques*, if you will,

—Or, even if you *won't!*)

Whenever asked, Picasso refused to divulge the secrets to his creativity and following suit impishly so will I!

The *Works* (*werke, les oeuvres*) are manifestly *there.* (*Here?*) On the page for the joy—*jouissance*—of the Reader. It was, after all, André Breton who said, "Let the words make love".

Reader, along with you, I sit back to read these strange works of Sotère Torregian, *someone* with whom I've been acquainted for some time: (French) Surrealist, Avant Garde American associated with "The New York School" (It was John Bernard Meyers of *Tibor De Nagy* Gallery in New York who introduced the name for a group of painters and poets gathered in the environs of Manhattan, New York, *circa* 1955–1967, where Yours Truly found himself between the years of 1963 to 1967)

I've been on the trail of this fellow, Sotère Torregian, for some time now, I'll admit, but have come to find out little of his real *persona* (Recall Jung cites the origin of *persona* coming from the Latin, "a mask"!) and have come to the conclusion that the poet remains an *enigma.*

THE FOLLOWING IS NOT AN APOCRYPHAL STORY BUT IS TRUE, BASED ON ACTUAL OCCURRENCE IN NEW YORK CITY (I *know*, because I was *there*) BUT YOU CAN CONSIDER IT APOCRYPHAL, IF YOU WISH.

It must have been sometime around the beginning of the year, 1966. Ted (Berrigan), having imbibed assorted "pills" and downed the same with a Pepsi, was walking with me in the environs of St. Mark's Place; both of us waxing nostalgic if at that hour—it was late evening—the lovely *Anne* (Waldman) might then be disrobing and we might catch a glance of her naked form near the window,—what a feast for the eye that would be! A chill in the air. Ted declared he had in mind to "steal some books" over at the Eighth Street Bookstore (maybe some of his own there, too, who knows)

En route, Ted suddenly blurted out:

"Sotère, you are a legend!"

"—*What!* what do you mean, Ted?"

Ted, laughing with his mischievous laugh) as was his wont when about to make a point:

"I mean you are a legend."

"Well, explain to me how that is; I don't get around as much as you do. You'd be more the candidate!"

"Ha Ha! I tell everyone that "Sotère Torregian" is a name Ron Padgett and I made up one night when we were both high and writing one of our major collaborations and we wrote the poems too!"

"You—you're not serious! (I can still hear the echo of my astonished voice on that cold, crisp evening in New York)

"Oh yes, I am! You can ask anybody you want"

"*Ohmigoodness*—No! What are you trying to do with me?"

At that moment Ted slaps me on the back and lets out his characteristic roar of laughter.

"Just kidding, man. But it could be, you have such an *unbelievable* name!—and that picture of you in the *Young American Poets!*—All kidding aside, man, you're O.K., you're a great poet, but, man, you're too *serious*, Sotère,—lighten up!"

That was Ted's by-word for me: "too serious".

That walk took place forty-two years ago, but I still see it and hear those voices vividly in my mind's eye

(Où *sont les neiges d'antan?*)

—Sotère Torregian,
   April, AD 2012
   Stockton, California.

Prologue

. . . *August, AD 2008 Somewhere* three marvellous lines are waiting to complete my poem)

—*There* is the key—the *enigma!*

"The *enigma* suffices"—Maurice Maeterlinck

"'Just be yourself,' he told himself in the beginning. Ah, but *what* self?"
—Ted Berrigan, *A Boke*

"messages d'amour égarés aux quatre coins du monde"
—Aimé Césaire, *Les Armes Miraculeuses*
(messages of love sent out to all four corners of the globe—translated from the French by S. T.)

Works, 1960- 1970

Death of a Poet

for Boris Pasternak (1890–1960)

How does the world go "on" when a poet dies?
The man next door (the husband) gets into his car
and starts his engine, about 8 in the morning, getting ready
for "work". His wife, the neighbour,
Mrs. Czapalinski, his wife, looks out
her window for a few moments; on Columbia Avenue the girls
idly saunter by on their way to school with textbooks
          chatting between bursts of bubblegum
(*They will hear the teacher's dour discourse*

On the process of onomatopoeia and trochaic in poetry;
also assigned diagramming a poem, "A B A B A", etc.)

Here in this room, it is only I
          who look on, a solitary,
who knows your name, who lives on

As the Sea goes on (even though far from my sight)
The trees hold knowledge beyond the human ken
The day is bright but will become cloudy later on
The room in Peredelkino
now barren but light continues to stream in
from the windows there. No one has discerned
          the Poet's secret in his remembrance of lost loves

Here the TV blares the words
of murderers (Those who govern the nation and those called
"distinguished" leaders of industry)
And *their* words are taken as "true"

1960

Waking Dream

for Patricia Neuhaus

"Quand io penso un gentil desio"
—Dante, *Canzoniere ix*

I stand on these rocks
          *klephtic souled

             And wait for you
        to defy with me
All that has been as "given"
to shatter logic and the "Idols of the Cave"
(Though alone in this empty house
      I sing "this song unto
           my own ears")

NOTE: * "klephtic souled". *Klephts,* bands of Greek bandit–poet resisters during the Turkish Occupation of Hellas (circa 1820s)

1960

A Sheet of Newsprint Goes Flying Past the Window

for Geneviève Del Sordi

The "eternal return": where I watch the street
from my window

        As they move forward and I remain
      behind
They have their knowledge and I
    have mine; that they (with their law books in arm
    and teachers' manuals *in this dark of fall*)
can never discern

Ah, Boreus!
do you bring news for those who have
ceased to dream; have you touched
her hair today

As she went forth from her door?

Unseen I sit here and look out. I have nowhere
to go today. But my poems invisibly
ride on this sheet of newsprint
as messengers

NOTE: Le nom de *Geneviève (sainte)* (AD 420–512) patronne de Paris
The "eternal return": myth of the eternal return. Eternal recurrence, posited
by German philosopher Nietzsche, that time is cyclical; the eternal return
of all things.

1959

Trois Poèmes Du Témoignage
(Three Poems of Witness)

for Diane Gugliotta

Presence

From this my coronation from the lily
so many books that stained my hands
$\qquad\qquad$ *"Presences"*
Love's stigmata spoken

$\qquad$ I asked the Stranger heaven's-
dolphin gliding on crow-sticks
'Do you *need* any help
$\qquad$ Is it hard for you with *those*?
—'Are you a Student?' *"Yes."* '*Student*
Of *what?* *"Nothing."* The world filled with rags in
$\qquad\qquad\qquad\qquad\qquad\qquad$ his eyes.

As he went forward
Ovulum of knowledge. I am a Stranger now
On so many roads. Even on the way home — —

Montclair

"My earth's only day of Spring, what have I known of you?"

Guarded
Absentminded angel
Montclair $\quad$ Scotch parties
$\qquad\qquad\qquad$ you hung naked
Unceremoniously $\quad$ from a tree
By your ankles and blew
$\qquad\qquad\qquad$ softly for the wind
No shamans in the wood
Near Eagle Rock

Your dilemma born on this rocky ground
sounded its clarion
                    There (No Ghetto
                              No Giotto devils
                                        but
          McCarthy demons still roaming)

To express the profoundest

People their plots cottages and painted stones
you know too well (Like the Youth of the Gerascenes)
          You gnashed yourself against the rocks
ready for another abandonment

The War God

          "To put back the pieces of the world"

This rage veered into absurdity

Out of green licorice.

Out of spiraled indifference
You came looking for me with the blonde-blooded monster
The God of War, #73 blazoned on his hatchet

He was friendly helping you try
To find me.

1963–1964

Miroir d'un Moment . . . (Mirror of a Moment)

for Joe and Rose Ceravolo

Turn face white in a morrow's margin
       air of aluminum
           Eyes that show brown secrets of pain
fated behind a common screen of venetian blinds
Cheeks cannot keep in the light their pouches weight
       of suspicion   I am energumène

Mannered in the house of a mirror.
       O better to live
Am I my own soul's gun runner?

And shall someone spell my dark — —

Complete   With their name penetrate
thus the honesty of   travelling my own Africa tearing
away at the tiger's outermost tint
    (*What stranger's moon must I
    fulfill?*)

O pregnant Puerto Rican women old and young!
O as graceful as gazelles pouring on green silk
                     making serene mad-
       ness in Bamburger's   Bargain Basement
Among the wild and worshipful forests
Of womankind

    (*What Stranger's moon must I
    fulfill*)

1962

<u>QUEEN OF THE NIGHT   ARIA</u>

Epoxy epoxy epoxy epoxy epoxy epoxy epoxy
epoxy epoxy epoxy epoxy epoxy epoxy epoxy
epoxy epoxy epoxy epoxy epoxy epoxy epoxy
epoxy epoxy epoxy epoxy epoxy epoxy epoxy
epoxy epoxy epoxy epoxy epoxy epoxy epoxy
epoxy epoxy epoxy epoxy epoxy epoxy epoxy
epoxy epoxy epoxy epoxy epoxy epoxy epoxy
epoxy epoxy epoxy epoxy epoxy epoxy epoxy
epoxy epoxy epoxy epoxy epoxy epoxy epoxy
epoxy epoxy epoxy epoxy epoxy epoxy epoxy
epoxy epoxy epoxy epoxy epoxy epoxy epoxy
epoxy epoxy epoxy epoxy epoxy epoxy epoxy
epoxy epoxy epoxy epoxy epoxy epoxy epoxy
epoxy epoxy epoxy epoxy epoxy epoxy epoxy
epoxy epoxy epoxy epoxy

So., 1965

The Newark Public Library Reading Room

for Calvin Forbes and for Philip Lamantia

I have a new home. A roaring Sparring Partner like a sunspot
Orifice for the grey membrane   theodicy and lexicon
    of my laughing years.
It is the Public Library of the Skull
Where every day round the clock poor old vagabond eccentrics
and alcoholics enter. The vagabonds
                jest with the librarians tell them
    their jokes lives and troubles
O Harlequinade!

And the librarians grow hysterical up their left sleeves
Until I can see a zigzag shape grinning and I know
these winos—I amongst them—are the real harlequins!
An old waif in breadline clothes and tattered hat reads at a table
            back issues of *Better Homes & Gardens*;
and from a strange periodical called *Gourmet* he righteously
                scribbles
frighteningly vast tracts on scrap paper and paper bags
as if the world depended on it.
I must get away from these harlequins.

Yet it is in this smudged lapidarium that I search for my Chanterelle

Between the resemblance and the divine image
It is my blood that flows down uncharted streets of
dreams   where in the monotone cleft
you are motionless between the resemblance and the divine
      image   unreconciled
There remaining   I find the eternal scansion with which
Eratosthenes measured the earth and the lips of the heavens

1965

André Breton

for Philip Lamantia

(Spectre of André Breton encountered in the Newark Streets)

As I am nostalgic   for BRETON
who pities the living
And Aragon who sits on his hair set afire
alights into the void on the train of winter engine No. X
tall fury   of transparent Lazarus
Breton's ingot eyes
preside over the castrati with your personal rocket
sound your words like the Red Desert
remove your stars again with flagellation
from your throat
song with the dust of Solomon's treasures
Bear incense to a backward people!

Knife sharpener of the Earth's crust of argentine
Fireman of the baleful stars of the pampas
Doorman of the night's murderous hotel!

        I can't pay my fare I don't have enough change

Vulcan's secret seagull's clang
Clown of Ishtar
On tamarind seas   spreading your ephemeral sails
André Breton!
I am here against a denuding wall
This is my last resort
My muse will write the scenage in its own blood

1965

9

On the Plain of the Flaming Giraffe (after Dalí)

for Barbara Anne Miller

On the plain of the hinterland
of a thousand drugstores   Where the sun
    is useless
goes the flaming giraffe
with his one eye tied to avoid
the bursting noise . . .

I stand inside the mirror and watch
          the reflections of days
come and go   far-gone reflections   retravailling themselves but
unmoved

My call to women, "Wild Bill needs you!"

Look you have frozen seals
My Son

From the "book of Harlequins"
I hear invisible applause in the background tomb of the sea

1966

At the Cedar Tavern with Frank O'Hara

"Nurse of stars"
—Paul Éluard

When you lose your job

                     wounds in the report of your unreal hair

two Ruthenians   hop skip and jump
from across the street
shake duplex hands and run
through a red streak violin

ascending

We   are on

      an infirm barge   held aloft by many voices
Of the blue tourniquet
Gyrasol
which I bequeath to you
as my necessary plenitude woodbin of error
my hands as semaphores
en passant
to your cries   of Medallion! Medallion!   We have no success
                                         with
disguises.   We carry   our eyes like tupelo
in a pail.

1965

Poem–Play in One Act: Absolute Panda

for Bob Rauschenberg

Theme music: Liszt's *Les Preludes*
(. . . *standing next to ice-cream wagon,* middle-aged vendor)
A girl points her finger away from her dream of ice cream

(*The scene shifts to* dark; then a spotlight on a centrally located miniature
house)

Arms, shovel in hands crash the miniature house with one fell swoop.

Sirens. A green scream. (i.e., green lights flash as the scream rings out

Playing cards are strewn under the body of a giant brown bear, wandered
into an urban area, shot by police. View of police kneeling over the
vanquished animal.

A Chorus:
"Absolute Panda! Absolute Panda! An illusion of the Absolute Panda!"

Emerging out of the body of the slain bear: a girl in white appears; she
has long hair and holds a fan, smiling
The girl speaks:
"Till the end of June."
Bear continues to be dead like a rug with orange juice spilled on it. An
anonymous person from behind the stage spills orange juice on the bear.

Music sounds. (Les Preludes)

A Voice:
"Ask for Carlos or Bill."

The scene shifts to two soldiers. One a generalissimo, the other a non-com
officer. Generalissimo plants a medal on the soldier. The soldier begins to
cry, holding a sign saying, "Curb Your Dog!"

The General shouts:
"Victory!"
The soldier:
"Boo-hoo."

There is a procession of all the characters back to the cadaver of the bear, with the girl in the lead; she holds a diploma. Procession pauses as she steps away from it and leans over the body of the bear, pinning the diploma on him.

Characters All:
"Absolute Panda! Absolute Panda! An illusion of the Absolute Panda!

At the Corner of Broad and Market Streets

for Anne and Lewis (Warsh)

On the love of my wife at this late hour

My breaths pass like an impossible thief
In a worn-out pawn shop (*Mont de Pieté*)

You are sleeping
A tunnel from my mouth exudes   "Montana"   A precipitous lineage Leaves

                              Chop Suey of Marines!
Ah, You is *a Gangsta* says the man

"Believe me

You is a Gangsta"

1967

From "Russian Hill"

"O Maiden   Sprung of water!"

In detestation of my travels
     Thunderherd   Maundy
Yami

Cupola
     Watermelon in the air
The birds take flight

The *cri* of Czerkowicz

                    . . .   . . .
Time of Census-takers . . .
Uphill to us

But you are loving as a sand dune All tresses of the dunes!

We are the first employees
In your Jules Verne country standing legs apart
Wide apart over the *Mare Tranquilium*
A shoe flies out the window   (*flop!*)
Your mother and father send up a distress signal
Of jewels they retire to bed like Alps

1967

The Ovine Identity of Shakespeare (A Protestation)

d'une profondeur astrale de méduses (astral depth of medusas)
—Aimé Césaire, *Soleil Cou-Coupé*

WE LIE MORE IN THE WAKE OF A LEGEND OF SHAKESPEARE THAN IN THE LIGHT OF HIS *REALITY*. We know the textual criticism, the laboured philosophies on the Bard's "ultimate meaning".—We know too much of Shakespeare and still not enough. We know of his wide influence; of *Hamlet, Macbeth, Romeo and Juliet*. We know he is the picturesque, often cited, *Renaissance Man*; yet we have been inflicted with him, *forced* to live with him, so to speak; *but we yet do not know him*. I need not stress the wide aura of his fame and influence, across the Continent and back again; from kingship to lowly peasant survivals; from love to hate; from Dylan Thomas (and his resonant *basso* renditions) and all the major poets of the English-speaking world . . . where Shakespeare reigns as a minor deity. BUT IS IT HE who reigns, more than the legend? *Where* is the *poet*, where is his life? ("The Shakespeare Question" has been thus debated for over a century.) What I shall pose is the Mystery of the Poet and universality of the Dramatist. (It is the latter that is more an infliction on us, much as the Bible might be so.) We may see the two thick volumes (*Shakespeare's Complete Poems and Plays* and the Protestant King James Bible, side by side, lying in wait to test our ignorance or our strength. Yet, as André Breton says, "EXISTENCE IS ELSEWHERE!" . . . How will we, then, know the real existence of the Poet as over against the decorum and dogma of the *Institution*, that is the Shakespearean Institution wherein teachers of English are the wardens over the student–prisoners? The poet, Dylan Thomas, says, in one of his poems— and it speaks universally of the poet and artist in society—"I in my intricate image stride on two levels." It is the level of life, the blood we must drink to vitalize ourselves. What level shall we chop down? That prison called the Institution of Shakespeare! Let the real Shakespeare be revealed to us: let us see his heart laid bare", his forrays into the depth of us. . . . Let us hear his devastated groans, not his chalk-board *exegesis* by an emotional cripple. Let the Poet be *revealed* let us attend to his level. Let the Bard come out of the coils that surround him!

—Shakespeare in the Woman that he loves! Why has he been abolished? IN THE NAME OF POETRY I MUST PROTEST!

One of his great characters, HAMLET, has been made the central core of the predicament of Modern Man; also, the "mad Dane" has become the symbol of madness . . . the Poet on the world stage

Or the world-stage in his soul. . . .

. . . running through the shadows of his own life, from action into dream, dream into action, meeting his inexplicable inheritance, the world; then meeting himself again as his own adversary, fighting the duel to the death, the *cri* of Poetry in the world. Penultimate of Life and Death.

HERE IS THE OVINE IDENTITY OF SHAKESPEARE! And we—we are part of the *Play-within-a-Play* put on by the mummers in *Hamlet*:—in the great belly of the Lascaux Whale: there in the gut is the OVINE Soul of the Bard, Let us then be seated and silent *therein* "We" *do not know him.*

Shakespeare is all the more to be honoured in his surrogate as his revealed Identity: SHAKESPEARE IS A SHEEP! The only *Ovine* to learn the English Language and so excel in it as to outrun all his contemporaries—to such a proficiency that he became the Supreme Poet of the English Language, setting its standards for ages to come.

THE REAL SHAKESPEARE WAS NOT A MAN BUT A SHEEP

(Now just think of the secret pride of ovines each time Mark Antony's oration is intoned!)

THAT OUR GREATEST ENGLISH POETS AS WELL AS THE WORST, OUR FINEST HUMANS AND NOBLE STATESMEN OF THE NATION, WHEN THEY QUOTE OR ALLUDE TO THE BARD OR WHEN THEY IN THEIR SPEECHES PRAISE SHAKESPEARE—PAY HOMAGE *TO A SHEEP*, whose bellows are more exalted than their claptrap. Thus our teachers teach the *Works*, the Collected Poems and Plays of the World's most celebrated (*though incognito*) cloven-hoofed Poet!

1967

Sneeze (Translated into Russian as Чпхátb!)

for "Uncle Kenneth" (Koch)

It's 10:30 a.m. already the traffic shouldn't be so heavy
A sneeze   cracks like a woodman's ax felling a tree
I call you your line is busy
If this is true then this is the sneeze heard round the world

Let us protect the sympathy we know   This autumn
the worms are rotting   in the dust
The minutes come by friendly with their fat dogs you can ask
any questions you want to. You   are on a flat land
The circle widens all about you It is the sneeze
the sky is its umbrella that laughs at everything I say
your young woman's body growing They shall come upon
a virgin land in a cactus garden And on the hand there it will be
written "They shall not shun"
Today your torches burn for the man who said, "Gosh, I spilled your coffee"
after being runned over by a car
A sneeze in time   saves . . . .

Others   change
It is I who remain the same

1967

ON THE BIRTHDAY OF
PABLO PICASSO ("Je Aime ce poème "

Today I ate a baked donut

I saw the woman who rebuked me in love

She was having breakfast with a hairy-man
  (One of the Boogy Woogies in Laurel & Hardy's Babes In Toyland)
Hoo ! Boogy Woogie !

There is nothing like a beautiful morning
When you don't care about the woman who has rebuked you
          in love
The fountains open up a pathway
Happy birthday Pablo
I walk over the path the fountains have made for me

Everything is imprinted with this sadness of nonconcern
All day I have been driven completely mad
By an imaginary hair on the nose
I would sound this clarion to you
Everything is imprinted with the sadness of nonconcern
And I am not concerned with my nonconcern
Although I wish I were somewhere else at this time
It is as if I were standing speaking with the gift of tongues
On top of a Lapland hound

                    Sotère Torregian
                    25 October 1967   (Picasso's Birthday
                     Palo Alto, Calif.
                    inédits

Crossing: San Andreas Fault, April 1968

for Martin Luther King Jr., 1929–1968, in memoriam

Yesterday cocoons whistled down from the trees
Like conga drums
Whose hands were silenced in sand.

                    In a portico reminiscent of the Alhambra
          I walked   wishing to be forgotten   only for a
moment

In the hot sun   in the cold fountain

With a slit down the side of the skirt

Assassinating lutes

        · · · ·   · · · ·

Today, at San Andréas Fault

The bullet
That killed Martin Luther King
O world on wheels   has pierced me   through

As the Fault pierces   the countryside   as the power-towers
              pierce the sky

The mute Braille alphabet of the Ocean shifts.

1968

Pour Chatterton

à Mme. Roséline Alríc-Cleaver

Un gibier né aéroplanes
Un gibier non un aeroplane
Mais donnes nous notre pain quotidien (*Intrusion*)
l'Écriture sur le mur
Si vous regardez ceci, vous êtes probablement en train de chier sure le pancher

Comme l'avatar moderne de Don Juan
    en enfer sait bien
qu' à son sujet
chaque poète moderne chante le même air
        Il joue avec lui-même
Ma soeur mon rouleau compresseur
Je mange une orange chaque jour pour déjeuner
Et cela est mon élégie
Les palmiers ne peuvent rien faire que chantonner
    "♫ À la lumiére de la lune argentée" . . .
Comme de vieux fous dans un pensionnat
Pendant que j'ai en ampoules infectées aux pieds
Tu peux   épier par la fenêtre,   sourire et dire bonjour

La parade non voulue des chants qui reviennent
    de quelque region oubliée de cervaux
soumettant enfin au grand ventilateur   suspendu du
    restaurant
Comme un homme guillotiné et qui observe ses dernieres
    sensations dans leur dernier mouvement

Les mains reconfortants des femmes
pathetiques comme de donner à quequ'un un penny
Chaques fois   que j'ouvre la
      fausse combinaison
          je porte encore
             les pantalons
          d'un mort

1968

Poem for Chatterton

Un gibier ne aéroplanes
A game not airplanes
But gives us our daily bread   (*Intrusion*)
The Writing on the Wall
If you are looking at this you are probably sitting on the floor

As the modern avatar of Don Juan
        in hell knows well
That about him
Every modern poet sings the same tune:
        He plays with himself

My sister my steamroller

        I eat an orange every day for breakfast
        And that is my elegy

Palm trees can do nothing but croon
        "By the light of the silvery moon" . . .
Like old fools on a pension

While I have infectious shoe-bite

You can peek in the window smile and wave

The unwanted parade of songs that return
        from some forgotten region of the brain
Submitting at last to the above revolving restaurant fan
Like a guillotined man who observes his last sensations
        making his final movement

The comforting hands of women
        pathetic like lending someone a penny

Everytime I open the
   wrong combination
    I still wear
      the pants
    of a dead man

NOTE: Thomas Chatterton (1752–1770) English poet, became saint of the Romantics. See the painting (depicting the poet's suicide) *The Death of Chatterton* by Henry Wallis.

From the French of Paul Éluard, "Belle Epouse"

Beautiful wife of memory
She rose from his bed
Like an entrance into history

1968

يا عَدُوَّتِج L' ADOU, The Woman–Enemy

for Linda Slotnick

I nibble on cookies in my office

And my brain is chased by an immaculate
    pillar with an automatic

Her hair the colour of the desert in its fierceness

To meet John Hawkes in Rhode Island

The French jewels of Amål Falluti
O Adou!
My enemy   أُعَدُوَّتِج

I saw taking refuge in a sandwich your double
                When I discover
                        her
She says, "That's all right. Everyone takes me for Someone else these days"
through her mouse-glasses

I want to cry for her
But I continue on my way

The many times I've passed unknowing

How soon your Cantabrigian house has stopped
singing
Every time I've passed it like the Egyptian Army in the Sinai
of 1966

In that way I meet you
You and your amazons who cry
        in their *manœuvres* bayoneting mirrors

1969

Chez Andre(i) (Codrescu) Era

"You Should have been a priest"

Today we're having beans and hot dogs and salad

Where there is   INK   there's   Hope

I WANT MY FOUNTAIN PEN   IT'S THE ONLY ONE
            WITH POETRY IN IT
I FEEL KINDA DRY TODAY   My mind isn't at
                          Palo Alto
                                    It's at *Siberia*

I don't like the flies that are eating
"ONCE AGAIN I HAVE NOTHING TO WRITE"

You are Don Quixoté, surely because you drink too much

            And you are blind
You are blind in the behind where it *counts!*
Count Tolstoi, for example, he
                          had no behind!
Ashcans sing my threnody
Abbott the Rabbit has a nasty habit
                                    of running away
            with the bread
In the Great Train Robbery
And hiding it in between bags of goldbricks
and gold coins
                and gold cops:
Fourth of July, you know how the Americans *are!*
I have to take the baby, *eh?*
Cop sirens with the toilet/flush my agony

The madder mad hatter came down the ladder
    with a TV antenna stuck to his head
It looks like
            he's madder

26

                    than when I left him last year
With a whole spear stuck in his cock
Shooting Bunny up to the
          moon — —

My Neighbour opened his window and called me "Madman!"

I opened it back and said,
                    "(You *called,*)
                    Madame?"

Sotère with Andrei, at Stanford, California

1968

On the Eve of the Moon Landing

for Kathleen

Day by day, London is sinking like a hissing diamond by the weight of its own tears. This while Bonnie, a youthful monkey blasted off from Cape Kennedy a week ago, pushing buttons and receiving food pellets for her efforts, slipped slowly into orbit

Dogs with mysterious passports come in the middle of the night
and chase you around cars
I'm not Flash Gordon I'm Buck Rogers
We must beware of imitating ourselves. The Red Star linen service
across the street sings a cradle song
by nature the cold hands of July as well as January

Martyriology of Spring on its translucent-paned doors

Thousands of GIs of the 1940s using the word "frig" for the first time in the "Theatre of War" causing a new wave from the *Lunar Mare Pamphilium*

The gardenias in your hat and the cactus in my fingers when they touch
Maskers pass the Cape Verdé Islands   in search of

The prize, entitled The Mouth of Truth   with my mouth

An old Black beggar with a turban approaches you and tears
off a piece of blank white paper and says:
"*This* is your future"

I wave Goodbye with my poor handless arm the mule and the sawmills
The cloistered nuns in the deserts of Arabia send you
a blackmail letter but we destroy it, counteracting their influence
A fascinating mission To challenge you to find a blade sharper than
     myself   To be naked in the middle of a thunderstorm in the middle
of a forest in midday We assassinate the TV weather Girl
who explodes into a parrot—*Sqwaak!*

28

Just as men land on the Moon.
When a lady sits on a horse, it's one thing, *but* when
a horse sits on a lady, well, isn't it cause for cutting flowers and leaves off
Lillies of the Nile—and sawing down and carting away a tulip tree?

Anyone so inclined to play the game
had better stick to the adolescent kissing brand of "Post Office".
A massive lock jamming is soon to be underway!
How is it we are always going separate ways
When always we are together,
            moving toward each other?

1969

"AT THE THRESHOLD OF THE FOUNTAIN OF YOUTH"
COLLAGE, 1969

On the Knocking at the Door in *Macbeth*

for Anne (Waldman)

~~Six o'clock
I smell the beach
without the beach~~

~~Six o'clock
I smell the beach
without the beach~~

Six o'clock
I smell the beach
without the beach.

1968

poème-objet : " In Her Image " , -- S. T. , 1969

Poème–objet: "In Her Image"

On the Planet without Visa

AFTER HOURS, *The Daily Planet* office closed, an unattached
hand comes out to put a record on the hi-fi, called "Everlovin'
Marylin" It seems no little girls are called Marylin any longer
With belligerent dips into fusillade, I was surprised
by the history of *The Daily Planet* talking to itself
Even stones make "heat" when they're rubbed together

A sense of sorrow comes over me upon encountering
a group of schoolkids playing in the late afternoon fall
Chanting "Red Rover, Red Rover"
Recognizing one of them will be a future bride . . .
Walking upon a road not yet paved
the tar still sticky beneath the tread of your feet

Ah here an even greater bank of sorrow, that of Art
Ha ha stuff the prodigy inside the violin case
    with a little dog

How survive the insolence?
That seem to speak French but it's only muttering
en anglais   English!
And when they get up are seen to be almost bowlegged!

That is, letters, telephone calls, CIGARS CIGARETTES
and other acknowledgements
While meaning to "uphold" actually unmasks the hero

In this dream where I'm lost in the smokescreen
thrown up by my own fame   The girl behind the check-out
counter at the store appears to be just returned from Paradise
as she lands in a mounted position onto the While Buffalo
Outside a picture window I walk from my past
it rains toasted birds from the sky onto the ground

As I watch the young woman in her golden ennui
enter the door of the limousine held open for her
by a suave male escort
I've arrived late and sensational

like a hustled diplomat of the UN
It may still be that there is another resolution

                    No matter whether I am a *raisonneur*
or vagrant denizen of a coffee house walking the night in
            an army-surplus trench coat in disguise
I vindicate the dead Masks of the Bambara ancestors live
through me

1971

Che Guevara

I find there is anachronism within me
A Third Law of Thermodynamics of a shrinking sun
Which guards itself
from the Pacific's sentinel –eyes
There are those who are commissioned to keep the Status Quo
on Earth (the burden of the poor's thus insured)
It's true my natural inclination is to prefer to be as much
as possible in the company of beautiful and lively women
Like the character of the eighteenth-century aristocrat the *Scarlet Pimpernel*
My shadow's always tested against the Cave

Of the coffee house! like the Wandering Jew with hearth burning

    inside him   with radio turned on full blast in his head
to ease him of his anonymity
and the world's misery

Yet forever Comrade I am a man like yourself with no home

I can never be at home in "this world" or in another
Its music divides my body from my soul

I search after each young woman who can be found
with her book open to the unfurled picture of Our Lady of Guadalupe

   . . . .

The concertina squeaks out from the depths of the Bolivian jungle

In a bit of asthmatic smoke   it says "I know how my life can be justified"

    Why, Comrade, you lived and died   and here is
a generation blinded by
its own *hum,* moving, rising, upward
like a helicopter I within it like a scrambled egg
it carries away both myself and the Mona Lisa's smile

(along with some other doubtful artifacts of the age)
coming toward you CHE with a need
for direction.
So we see these signs in the gothic monuments in the public

lavatories effaced with graffiti. A moon part dark
and part bright side   which is where the entourage
of the voiceless move toward you
Where they *become*
One with a voice in the image of your
                    death at Villegrandé *(perfume of*
Michelle Rey's Parisian bellbottoms in
the night) vision of a rainy windshield   your eyes
drenched in formaldehyde

Thus, the slow dark caravan moves across Asia Africa and the Americas

When I walk in the night and look into
lighted cellars I see old unredeemed legs looking like hambones
sing with wizened voices: *"Hambone Hambone where ya bin'"*
calling at me as I rest seated in a wayside hothouse nearby
A giant beanstalk sprouting upward hatched from
a classic torso centerpiece
I watch it spring into the sky
as I sit there breathless

With my album of old loves and those that are to be
I'm weighing lighter and lighter
The Nightwatchman comes with jangling keys
to lock all the doors
I rouse myself from my **cauchemar*
"Preventing the Death of the Cities" I carry a Christmas tree
As the last really "great"
                    Comedian of the Silent Screen . . .

But here with CHE I find my destiny
O Refugees!
O you who sleigh in your sorrows on automatic weapons!
Palestinians Men and Women of the *ANC* Mozambiquiens

36

You are now my homeland

    wherever you are
                           roaming
You take my language and my race
and whatever I have known of beauty.

NOTE: * *cauchemar, French,* nightmare

1970

"Duck Soup" with Mengistu Lemma, in San Francisco

I'm not in good form today

The devil cut the rope and the saint plummeted 1000 feet
Then flew off with six wings on his back.
Ah, *Duck Soup!*
In a miniskirt I ate with a poem in Ge'ez for *sauce*
Confucius say: HAVE DRUNK INSIDE
               (Bad for Health)
I—I'm in love With you O fire escapes
—Round and round we go
"O Brown-Skinned Girl" don't wait for me; I go
                          to City of Hankow
    The Angel—arrested for flying over Times Square
with Barbarella (Jane Fonda) in his arms shooting peas
from a pea shooter at "hard hats" and businessmen below
I'm asking

            The City, dressed as a beggar, who am I?
Plastic pants are now creeping out the door of the bar,
    but there's no escape
Except through the gate
of green-headed dragons and fish

Playing the street signs as guitars to the moon I can't see

— —"But! I was in Houston and saw it there

Ah ha, there's the fire escape! Where's it go to?

To the top of the moon! Dear Passerby
    I find myself at a loss
for words, I mean I think I'll drink some more beer
Is everything O.K.? Yes, but not with the science
of sexology. She always comes back in that miniskirt
and well, cultivated smile. *Mais Oui!*

Makes me feel like a second-story man that the State of Israel
aims to shoot down (Missed again, guys!)
My Armenian-sounding Friend
                                        Who
can't change his spots! so to speak. Tell me,
am I not now transported
to Harar drinking beer and wine with *Rimbaud himself?*

Quick call for the Ark! (rather encumbered
    on the heights of Mt. Ararat between Turks and KGBs)
                    There are many
Tasty Middle Eastern delicacies here in the City
Also in Cairo—just don't ask there for *matzohs!*

Yet the smiles of beautiful women   always vanish
when I receive them
I'll sing along with
Robert Redford and Paul Newman
"Raindrops keep a-fallin' on my head"
You should open your umbrella, then but choose not to!

1970

NOTE: Poet Mengistu Lemma, friend of the poet, disappeared in
Ethiopia in 1976 during the dictatorship reigning at that time. Ironically,
the dictator's name was also Mengistu!

Works, 1970 - 1990

La Cadenelle
(Selections from a Novel in Progress)

dedié à Mlle. Nadine Favre, Marseilles, Fr., et pour M. Jean-Louis Armand

"Mademoiselle Soubirou" ("Queen of the Forest")

33.
    There's no Victor Schoelcher here for me
no one to write me out of this slavery
                   (of the continuous lust for your body . . . *Nadine*

34.
I even feel strange feeding my own locks

35. (You are in St. Louis, Mo., now)

    And where is this surprise I tell my friend the Navilles the Crêvé-coeurs the white shadows of the world "American music"—the latest jazz"—which is your delight—still plays on without you in St. Louis (the young French girl tourist touring *l'Amerique*) What would the Marquis de Sade have to say (I admit I've imagined you there as the female novice in the pages of his *Sodom*) as part of our foreplay) there but *Whoopie* while the tears rolled down the eyes of the Afro-American trumpeter and drummer while the music sacrifice them as you sacrificed me sacrificed the sun before I could look twice in the body of man in the flowers the seas the mountains the whole frame "A bitter*something in the mid-most hours" this desire
    **un quelque chose acerbe*

36.
    Whose is the young woman's face playing "Ports of Call" with the California Youth Symphony Orchestra floating like the strum of a harp over this televised water for but a moment? Is it you when you were younger and your passions were just being learned by you like a book of the fabric of Valencia oranges *a book of hours I now read?*
    The Flamboyan tree is jumping around like a nut like African dancers one sees all attired in habits of hay. But the Flamboyan—you having given it your happiness (*ton plaisir*) *has made itself* into a *carte postale* and stuck itself into my left shirt pocket

37.

  IS IT the sensation of the water pulling me in as if I were a "message in a bottle" *to you O Cadenelle?*

38.

  where lifting my eyes to the heavens I see a dank boarding house unopened letters on the mantle where one might easily kill one's self in a "Song without End"

My memory mixed into the evening as you prepared our desert *bananas flambées*

1971–72

The Last " New York " Poem

My flashy red tie
my friends say
always precedes me
when I enter a room
is nostalgic about New York .
It 's a problem to live in a " rural area "
and still write about New York
But even if New York disintegrates there will always be
New York   in my tie.
What else is there beside New York ? I 'm like a fisherman
telling the fish a fish -tale. It 's best to love New York
when you ' re out of New York maybe

Hi ! Good Morning !
There 's a whole New York Construction Co. in
my tie

The cement -mixers are in my tie
Frank O ' Hara is in my tie
Gibralter Life Insurance is in my tie
Along with Fifth Avenue and its workmen
and " First-nighting "

                              sometime summer (?) 1971 --S. T.

for Bill Berkson

45

At San Juan Bautista, a Thousand Years of the Persian Empire on TV

for Maria of Teatro Campesino, wherever she is . . .

Ah, you caught me unawares on my island of doubt

These kind of meetings are the things

That created the Wyoming Desert, perhaps

And then the silences of the adobe of the Pueblos
your smile as you appear
before me stalwart yet yielding   to abolish
          all the bullets of the *Rualés* in 1911
the kind of scream that stays with you from the plume
of Quetzlcoatl's temple long after you've left Mexico
hiding still in the morning mailboxes
in your eyes   Where on the screen I watch the long caravans
of the 16th-Century satrapies on American TV
in a parade of a thousand years of the Persian Empire
on their splendid mounts all in their luster before Queen Farah
(*These are the last days of the Shah and his reign*)
In the letter I've received it asks where's the "fracture
of my irony and beginning of my agony"
          (*The Great Gate at Kiev*)   How is it
Mussorgsky's "Pictures at an Exhibition"
Always seems to play
          on the radio on my birthday
My lithe saltimbique   My filly-mime

Headlines in the newspapers on the day of my birth June 25, 1941
("Europe a disaster area")

Everything I do is supreme, that is when I can
be indifferent to it all

As Lorca in the tradewinds

46

But it's now for *our* one moment in *l'histoire* as I kiss
you *Agitprop Danceuse*
from Oaxaca
Openings of space blossom with your
grace wherever I go!

1973

In a Coffee House and in a Car:
An Interview with Sotère Torregian

by Becky Morgan for *The World* magazine's "World Interview Issue" edited by Anne Waldman. Published by The Poetry Project at St. Mark's Church in 1974.

Dear Becky,

Hello! Again. It was so nice meeting you today! "My life" is so hectic—thrown to the winds; I live at the mercy of the wind. My heart is flung to all passing strangers who walk in day and in night (*Nous Sommes*) *we are* thus all wayfarers on this (our) planet: and through these doors of hours we meet. I sit here in a restaurant after my daughter Janaina's appointment with the dentist! (Ouch!) Assyria is so far away from me, my Assyria, with the daughter of Ashurbanipal encaged in snow. O window of the snow! (I shall never see her again.) I am thrust now *in this world*, always seeming to *retrace* my lost steps. (Les pas perdus)

My four-year-old daughter, Janaina, and I are making *a picture poem*—so she's alternating with different *color pens*=red & blue . . . yellow (etc.)

I cry now for the deserted castles left in *KUSH* and in Assyria. And *also the deserted castles left in all of our lives!*

For these moments, you have asked me the following *and I respond*!

(you ask) What is "My *Reality*"? (Ah, that word!)

And now that my daughter, Janaina, and I are at home, in the curtains of the rain, now I am more "settled" and can think of what we spoke at our meeting . . .. I cannot write or speak without the dreams that lie within me, so that is why my "discourse" may seem somewhat strange to you, a little "scrambled" with images. But when we dream our images and words and sensations are in that same order; it's only when we wake, and the process of logic begins its workday in our heads, that we think we have experienced something "strange" in our dreams, but this is the deep life of the Poetic in all of us, in you, too, Becky, although unacknowledged,—and also in the life of your young son. I recall telling him (in the dentist's office) to dream and there he would find poetry and as well the truth of his own being (*l'*être) When you dream, too, Becky, you, too, will find what you are looking for in life, the world of night and day, the conscious and subconscious minds meeting.

We are in a sense kept prisoner by the world of the everyday. Romeo and Juliette fought the world of the everyday and its constrictions of the society in which they lived, declaring the Freedom to Love. Despite what apologists say, the world as we know it does not really understand the nature of Beauty and Passion and those who have been their forerunners. . . ... In the darkness of our hustle and bustle, these things I affirm with you—and Shelley declared the same until his skiff was shattered on the shore at Viareggio. . . . Ancient poets of my ancestors,—Arabs, Armenians, Ethiopians, Greeks, Moors, Troubadours—and lately my compères the *French Surrealists!* ask to keep the flame of the Marvellous, *Le Merveilleux*, and this I do, even at the risk of my life, but I keep it and pass it unto you,—all the poets of the world pass this sense of the Marvellous to you!

In effect, you are its energizer—poetry is not done apart from you—as in your own night your Woman's beauty confronts the Unknown and the Known . . . we let you know we recognize your integral reality, wholeness,— yes,—eros!—to remind you that beauty resides within you and without; that Love still lives in the world . . . that *shadows who see the delicacy of your hands as you speak . . ..* I have an inkling how difficult your life must be with school board meetings, trying to communicate with people who do not understand. During these times of stress, I hope you will remember these words of a poet.
—À VOUS, YOURS, S. T.

[1) Tell me of your heritage?
2) Is your "knowledge" learned or felt/dreamed?
3) If artists do/did not feel *alive* would they be as creative?
4) Is wisdom tapped or innate?
5) You talk of the West. Is the "East" a better place?
6) How do we recapture the beauty of human relationships? me *seeing your beauty.*
7) Why did I offer you a ride?
8) Is a poet really a "change agent"?
—"Reality of destiny"

(The above in her own hand, are the questions, posed by Becky Morgan to the poet, Sotère Torregian]

Q. Tell me of your heritage?
A. In the Book of Love of Ibn Hazm, *The Risálá*, there is the story of my "heritage." One day outside the walls of Baghdad, a beautiful young woman left her handprint on the wall, whose cement was not yet quite dry. A young man saw it and fell madly in love with the girl, *without having ever seen her*, resolving to trace that *handprint* to the end of his days. So her handprint was left on the walls of my heart, and I have searched her always. *She* was once the daughter of King Ashurbanipal of Assyria, and then a handmaiden of Lebanon, a Nubian

slave, and an Arabian water bearer in Sicily. In the book of Joseph Sheban, my Middle Eastern "heritage" can thus be researched. But my "heritage" is the moments of our meeting. My "heritage" is the shadow that *André Breton* gave to me:—and all the poetry in the world—and to you, same heritage! Surrealism gave to me my heritage and opened up my world of dreams. Assyria, Palestine-Lebanon,—*Nubia (Kush/Ethiopia of the Queen [Makeda] of Sheba)—gave to me my blood. My blood and my dreams met. And now they would rescue the beauty in everyone. And yet, in seeing you, my head bows humbly before Beauty, and my smile goes to all those I meet: therein, too, is my "heritage," which you help my to implant in the clouds and in hearts.

Q. Is "Wisdom" tapped or innate?
A. Wisdom is a window we can open in the sea. We must be navigable, that is, seaworthy. The beauty of eyes, hearts beating, the symmetry of breasts, the magic we make of each other's bodies: the way we "see." "Wisdom" is born of Desire. It is not in an Institution but in a discovery: it is the fire conveyed of that discovery. It is walking from your shadow into your love's shadow. It is taking 3,000 years' work of dream with you and remaining all the more new for it each time.

Q. You speak of "erotic energy." What is most important to you, actual sex,—that is, as the current term has it, "scoring," or the *encounter* itself?
A. I should think the actual *encounter* itself rather than the "scoring." The *encounter* and its mystique is what I find most fascinating in my relations with Women—and it really holds in itself the true surge erotic energies, and is a prelude to all things to come. The greatest poetry—q.v., Petrarcha, for instance—was written on inspiration of the life mysteries of *the other* person, rather than any physical description of what went on in the bedroom. Of course, this erotic poetry too has its own grandeur—as we see in the Persian erotic miniature paintings, but this art had already *a cosmology that was in place.* Ours, in America, is completely out of place and virtually nonexistent. (Hence, the equation of eroticism with what is called "pornographic" in modern western culture.)

I always love to meet new women! I find the *encounter* with them exciting: I like to sit for hours and see their beauty mingle with their minds at work, but I mean to sit and listen, to actually *learn* from them, the experiences that are most meaningful and that they wish to convey as feminine persons. It's the *encounter* that holds the stars of the Marvellous. (Le Merveilleux, in French) Sometimes I've dreamt of myself as a fashion photographer, because I relish the "mystique" of woman, her variousness, because there's a certain joy in it that the somberness of the male world with its "getting and spending" attitude is oblivious of. I think we must recapitulate life's mysteries in reconstituting the Primal Androgyne again.

Q. "Primal Androgyne"?
A. The sense of my entire conversation revolves around it, as you'll see.

Q. Why did I give you a ride?
A. One sees many lives going by like satellites. They open for a moment & then they close—and go from you: This life did not go from you—it opened to you & embraced you.

When you wanted to open yourself there were many who heard you: Van Gogh heard you. Gaughin heard you. Ishtar heard you. Assyria heard you: The clouds heard you; but they were mute and I was in their place. That beauty came to belong to us alone/

Q. How do we recapture the beauty of human relationships?
A. From the tenor of the question, I knew you had roamed, searching, opening, extending your hand. You saw many lives go and come before you. You expected something more: the beauty of your reality to be recognized. That's not what happened.

So I too have had fragments of the song and asked completion of the song.

Q. You talk of the "West." Is the *East* a better place?
A. The "East" & the "West" go past each other
& they ask the same question: *What is the East?*

  In the same way people ask
What is Poetry & they
pass it every day.

So, when reading a good part of this dialogue, some people will think we have not been speaking of Poetry *proper*, but they will have been mistaken completely. They will have to come back and readjust themselves into their shadows again.

Q. Is your "knowledge" learned or felt,—dreamed?
A. A year or so ago I knew nothing of this, our meeting, our words shared. You did not feel my hand upon your hand as we exchanged amenities. And now here you are, saying you are "saturated" with me! this is (a form of) knowledge. And your Woman's beauty flows into my vessel waiting to be filled. This is "knowledge" (obviously not that which western philosophy has sought to define)—this is beauty—*l'Hasard Objectif*—of Objective Chance,

the world's design bringing you toward me and me toward you, when we least expected such an occasion. Your day complements my night; certain poems prefigured you. And the way your magnetism shaped the filings on the curtain of day and night into the sunburst of my shadow: I then opened that door that appeared before me in human silhouette and it was you who stepped forth, in a reddish-brown pant suit, open-toed shoes, and your hair cut to shoulder length. The hemispheres of dream and reality meeting, interchanging, creating new horizons . . .. it took 5,000 miles before we knew this, yet the "knowledge" was—is—within us, civilisations of Africa, the Middle East, Byzantium, there, *intérieur*, waiting. When I was fifteen years of age I was transfixed by the music of *Borodin*, the music readapted to become the musical, *KISMET*, and the song, "This Is My Beloved," (adapted from Borodin's *String Quartet*) I didn't know then you were singing that song but now I know. *Poetry knew all the time.*

"Knowledge"—as opposed to the concepts of the philosophers—is for me composed of Eros, Dream, the Conscious, and Unconscious in the world: Knowledge bears the flame of Passion, *extending* this Passion to change the world for the better. Charles Fourier, whose thought was revived by the French Surrealists, elevated Passion in his *Theory of the Four Movements*. Even Jesus spoke of Passion. Marx spoke of it. Breton exalted it. (See his *l'Amour Fou*). And therein through all their words have I been led. The Dynamic of Hope. Logic is for the practical affairs of the world that need mechanical means to implement them. "Socrates is mortal"—so goes the syllogism, ad infinitum. Love poetry is for the *inutile* that which deserves honour and beauty in and for itself as its own activity and spontaneity. Logic is to run the motor cars of the world (with the diagram of the engine, exhibiting its vital parts); Love poetry is to run the motor of the human spirit. In the confusion of Love and Logic we see the morass that society sets before our gaze. Thus, exercising his spirit of freedom, Gauguin went to Tahiti, somehow anticipating the alienation of our own day. But there is no longer a Tahiti. There is one on the map, a place called by that name, owned by France. But there isn't the Tahiti Gauguin sought after. There is really no "place" which is really left to us any longer but to find refuge in ourselves, in our own inner Tahiti! It is there we must re-create our sense of *knowledge*—and love within ourselves. The French Surrealist poet, Aimé Césaire, of Martiniquien descent, says in one of his poetical works, "J'habite un voyage de mille âns." As point of information, see André Breton's *Ode à Charles Fourier.* . . .

Q. If artists didn't feel *alien* would they be as creative?
A. I think of the poet as something of a priest, whose religion is that of the wind. The world is my parish. I want to see how my parishioners—so to

speak—are doing. This encounter sets up the possibility for poetry. I hide behind clouds and sometimes I emerge where I am least expected: I emerge from the mask that is my self, from the dentist's office, from a sandwich-shop counter. The wind then gives me my vestments, energies of all beautiful women who dream day and night, for I am but their shadow, during the rain in November when they're driving along in the shopping center: I emerge to them the wind takes away my vestments then and says, "Okay, you're on your own now, kid; go on." And I go, not knowing where I am going or whom I may encounter, I stand there somewhat befuddled a little like holding my hand to my mouth, in front of people. I'm without any clothes on. Sometimes, Tammouz, my ancestor, who came from the mountains of Lebanon, retorts to the wind, "Silly!" and gives me some clothes. Then I can talk to you.

Q. Is the poet really a "change agent"? *q.v.,* **"reality of destiny"**
A. The poet is the mediator that appears in those agencies of change. Dreams and their negation; liberation from societal institutional restraints—and its negation. The poet Rene Char wrote:
>   "In the cockle shell of the anvil
>   lives the lone poet
>   great wheelbarrow of the swamps"
(Translated from the French by S. T.)
The poet is the *ferial door* of Plato's *maniké* and *mantiké*, meaning the thin line between madness and genius.

Q. "Ferial door"?
A. Instead of praising the beauty of a woman's body they talk about the poetry of—cars! Ugh! That's why the poet must be as the ferial door in this day. There are monstrous ersatz-false troubadours—Advertising Agencies— that legislate beauty. In short, Poetry is not allowed to come to you, given the status quo. But you must strive toward your own self-liberation. We must be the liberators of the dream as well as the social polity. You cannot believe in Love, or Poetry, and continue to be in the status quo. Romeo and Julliette were Revolutionaries (we will omit here their eventual ends, which shouldn't have had to happen): it was they who made Shakespeare the Poet, not vice versa: they were interdependent in widening the circle of Love and Poetry. The circle comes to us:—the "reality of destiny".

It so happened this afternoon, while I was waiting for you outside the coffee house where we were to meet, I stood quite still, with my foot up on a table there outside, thinking. A woman-friend then passed by and laughed: "Hey there, are you *The Thinker* of Rodin?" "I don't know but that if you stand there long enough you'll turn to stone!" I didn't know the meaning of that statement in my life until now. I *was* stone. It was you who then came and breathed life into my immobility and I became vivified again. That unknowing statement my French friend, Mlle. Pauline Baggio, was meant as a jest but it was a presage that we would live a complete day of poetry in each other. It was then also that I could how *Nadja*, in Breton's book of the same title, could see the wind blowing blue, because thereafter, my whitened statue saw the wind blowing blue, as you came and "turned me on",—into life, un autre fois, yet again.

The Two Butterfly Lovers

"Hello, up there!" "Halloo, down there! say the Two Butterfly Lovers. "Hi, Friday!"

"*Who's* Friday?"

"*You* are, of course, Friday. I've given you the name Friday" "Oh well, okay, who're you, then?" "I'm Thursday, remember?"

"Where do you live?"

"I live in the Golden Pavilion and that's my song"

Meanwhile, inside the Pavilion of Lions, Malamute dog, Michael, was drawing a picture of the two butterflies kissing. He was very pleased. He sang the song of the Golden Pavilion. At the moment the Two Butterfly Lovers were flying one was ahead of the other (so they couldn't play "leapfrog" in midflight) They saw the castle nearby. They settled there to have lunch. After lunch "Thursday" and "Friday" went for a short walk; on their way they saw millions of butterflies cavorting The sky was pink with some purple and blue. The sky said nothing

The Two butterflies went piggyback. They lived happily ever after and had lots of babies. They slept together in the castle of the Golden Pavilion. The mirror in the castle said: "You kids let go of your hand holding for just a little while so you can go to bed!"

Then, in the morning, the Two Butterfly Lovers, Thursday and Friday, had fish and rice for breakfast. They went out to pay a visit to 'Michael", the blue-eyed Malamute, who was happy to draw their pictures once again. Having been invited to have dinner with him, the butterflies after dinner fell fast asleep. In their dreams the butterflies saw two golden swords. In Thursday's dream one of the golden swords flew after Friday. Friday, the first butterfly, woke up suddenly in the middle of the dream and went into the kitchen for a glass of water. Drowsy, he stayed there until about five o'clock in the morning because the dream had been so frightening.

Outside, with the sunrise the castle was turning bright purple

Now awake, both butterflies left the castle, turning back to glance at it one more time as they flew away. The Two Butterfly Lovers took off their clothes and went swimming in the stream. It happened to be that a passing wanderer-guitar saw the two swimming naked it played its strings. Song was born in China.

—Sotère Torregian, 1974, with Tatyana Torregian, age 7

Woman of the Texas Panhandle, 1938,
Dorothea Lange

for Barbara Capell Lawrence, painter

"Another day Another dollAH." People travel their life's way on such phrases by the light of the sun by the light of the moon from their childhoods to their deaths Thirty years ago I remember the older women on blue afternoons repeating this phrase simultaneously shrugging their shoulders as they stood on the magic carpet of everyday, which took them around the corner in town. As blatantly as my daughter has just kicked over an anthill as I ask her to define the word "sea" Always the word "sea" As I am going along lighting the candles on the acolytes of Spring have forgotten to light

So *"Another day Another dollAH"* And the poor blue women come back again circling from around the corner now sad still standing on their suspended magic carpet mute before me, shrugging their shoulders, saying "Another day Another DOLLAH" . . . .. like the Apostles' clock high above the town-hall of Nuremberg striking the hour going in one end of the cloud and out the other out of sight, beneath is a desert blowing nameless marriages Only a minute photo of the mosquito with fluttering eyelashes blows in the sand. He plays tennis for recreation.
IT'S that mosquito that has drowned in our love And I tell you in my silences madmen tell me his story every day . . .

A kangaroo appears out of nowhere to watch the women in the cobalt blue above—*O kangaroo kangaroo*! how like the fleeting smile of a woman in a car you are! Sweet and clear below like the last poet on earth watching a night without wind.
Either of virtue or of mischief.
Smiles are not afraid. They return like killers back to normalcy Now with wind now without (wind) I am able to open this treasury
Among the wild red rocks and running beasties inside a top hat in the sleep of the blue-vaulted town. Only when I remember and have before me the women sadly returning from their magic carpet ride with the phrase "Another day Another *dollAH*"
And that the clouds take young wives these days and that is the secret that keeps the clouds ever youthful

1974

We Meet the African Prince

for Fr. Richard Del Affrim of Ghana

The girl having the operation on her leg doesn't know the African Prince. She's located in a modern hospital with gates that automatically close Closed out is the name Kwamé Nkrumah whom she does know loves her from afar O my Friend, Kwamé, you prince who has made of every African a prince or princess And has bestowed upon us the same So that the girl can talk to plants, along with other in the sunset where paper aeroplanes may be flown out the window anonymously

But she really knows the African Prince in her heart of hearts for to be loved is to be included in the "great drama" of Life "Styles" usually change the Prince was waiting for her outside the entrance Where a(n) hundred novels are "known" and read Where cloud-sweeps are watched by many. Where, on a Saturday night a young woman dances to the *reggae beat* and proclaims its incitement to the "Ruling Class" furniture you can make classics shown off Summer antique *Concours d'Élegance* I can hear the reindeer getting ready up on my roof for their workday It's dawn. My reputation in the halls of Justice heard in my mother's heavy breathing in her bedroom next to mine

In the hour of telecommunications Africa wakes Joan Miró's Antibes . . .
"Ah,
says the shower of Zeus on Europa, "Is it the birthday of the world's richest man?"
Today I am the answer. My serenity of handkerchief's
allows me to do everything after our meeting thus
in an "unhurried and easy manner" (rather atypical, I should say) Nostalgia of abaloné (the shells stolen from the rim of our home on Alpine Rd.) My friend ardent admirer of the *Book of Kells's* illumination My African Prince within you you preserve and love all that I have loved storybooks' blush at the word, "Épargne"
Then so many times a young girl takes your hand for guidance on the "slippery slope" of life And so the distance two houses with faces of the masks of Tragedy and Comedy The words "Put 'er there", overheard

1975

With Lita Hornick and "Bear"
at Trader Vic's, New York

You can't climb the ladder of Success

                With your hands in your pockets

                    Absence
       (sometimes) makes the heart grow fonder (and wider)
A woman's
        curiosity is as great as a man's
Good wife and good health
        is a man's best wealth

            "A very precious possession
       will soon be yours"
Something learned
       Everytime   the book is opened
Why so short a course
         having so long a lease
Don't drink the water, Sotère, the fish make love in it
Terreur
No one will ever find   the key   to ME
I feel the same way

Dawn Sounds (The House on Alpine Road, Menlo Park, California)

I am shaving   by the open window
My .32 automatic nearby rests on the bathroom sink

For any Peeping Tom who happens to peek
It's the day after my birthday   I'm beginning
    to think I should re-adjust
the Calendar (subtract some years)

Today's Before and After
(My birthday, that is)   But that would make mentioning
my "birthday" in poems boring
The Mask of Atibón Legba my birthday present from Haiti
does a headstand by my bed
Troughs filled with water and yeast for catching
    whirligigs (Buff Groff's suggestion)
I approach
a New Era   Ophelia

filled with the memory   of your porcelain body
Now can I catch up on some sleep (?)

WAKE UP! The Poetic Seismograph shouts
        Don't worry
People who live the longest are those
who are loved
Oldest Georgians   are 108 120 and 168, respectively
and are married imbibing vodka and red wine still!
Poets, come alive again take your novitiates not in hothouse writing
    classes but in hospitals and prisons
        At 6 p.m. and 1 a.m.
      the "real" zones of life
A train with commuters passing a prisoner behind bars weeps
    as the train goes by
At 6 p.m. and 1 a.m.
I watch your face speedily go by in a train
I don't even know your language

For Ted Berrigan in Chicago: Chicago Fantasia

Collaboration between Tatyana (age 10) and Sotère Torregian (age 36), 1977

for Ted Berrigan and Alice Notley

cars go by in the night. To the dreams in
my head. Men and women are dancing around having a ball drinking
whiskey and wine with party hats on　　　　　　　　At a party *in Chicago.*
There's a guy named "Chicago" at the party. They made a speech for him &
said Why don't we name this city "Chicago"! After the "party" there was
another party. A horse with one eye, whose name was "Fred," was there; also
a sheep with one leg, & a cat with five legs. The one-eyed horse had a
hangover. The song they were singing: *"Freddie, Freddie, sunset Freddie, never
let me cry!"* The headlines said in the night edition

"Friends of one-eyed horse have party." The "populace" of Chicago said
I don't believe there's such a thing! *Ted Berrigan* got the newspaper & read
the news. "A one-eyed horse in the newspaper!" said Ted. "Cookie eats cookie
monster," says *Alice. Ted and Alice rush off to Bob Yuban's Bar. In May I'm
sleepy enough.　　　Ce gentil petit animal, peut être découpé. Il y a 7 autres
amis que vous trouerez sur d'autres paquets de mes rêves. Clouds, also
present, at the gathering say, "We'll rain on them tomorrow."

NOTE: * Alice Notley, poet, 2nd wife of Ted's.

Cesar Chavez

Quadro portrait of his visage that rises here
Are you windward or leeward to give direction
In this interstice
I find myself in a bar of apes and near-men where
they rail against the Boycott
HUELGA Children of the Sun of Atzlán
I vow
To you the courage of African Slaves
    in the Atlantic crossing
And it will speak your name   CESAR CHAVEZ!
For Washington who stirred the spirit
of Revolutionary Struggle La Lucha!
throughout the then-known world Splendour of
bronze masculinity and femininity
O in unison

        I shall still stand in their midst
Red and gold flags reading in the October wind the first
moment Lenin addressed the Soviet that same mystery and fascination

Quadro portrait of his visage that rises here
Are you windward or leeward to give direction

The Shaman (Medicine Man Crow Dog Ambassador of the Sky

Each place where I have walked
have ever walked
Carrying with me silence of the Valley of the Qadisha (**Liban*)
And that of Boston Commons (1770) Crispus Attucks's *cri*

In Red Square or in Mississippi yet another Station
of the *Via Dolorosa*
Quadro portrait of his visage that rises
Are you windward or leeward to give direction

       where empires have risen and fallen vanished
and melted into
Earth   Air   Wind   Water   Fire
From out of your brown   *Liberador* like Bolivar
the dove flies there   agonied whinney of the horse
in Picasso's *Guernica*   (which I will ever allude to its siren
    sounding ever inside me)
Wherever I may be

Homo Faber! Man- and Womankind, the maker

Diego Rivera's *Rockefeller Center*
Murals erased yet where Marx continuously points to
the opened pages of his book *Das Kapital* to the despoilers
The Vision now blossoming into the family CHAVEZ
And the Children of The Sun of Atzlán
Again
      It is now the day breaks and the shadows flee away
Before the Marchers
bearing your ensign   CESAR CHAVEZ
Quadro portrait of his visage that rises
Are you windward or leeward   to give direction

NOTE: * *Quadro,* Spanish, painting (portrait)*; Liban*, French, Lebanon

Letter to Shelley Scott Lustig, New York, 1985

"I walk into my apartment and there's a homeless guy camped out in the vestibule" —Shelley Scott-Lustig

So that you might turn to "look within"

These converging paths   wrested
            from the objects of

                  occurrence where someone is chilled just
enters the room and warms himself at a stove.

Beauty's ties reach into the essential "ground"

    In a courtyard in Athens horses of afternoon pull away
from Gianni Ritsos's shadow   fascists have their own
doppelgangers to stare at
                        (*Je vous dis*
                              I say to you
There are sacred phrases in Ethiopic which are due here
but have since lost somewhere in my *cahiers*
But let it be noted

            "LUCY" and her kind *adapted*
on the lakeshore of Hadar, becoming thus
for the sake of us   "*sapiens*"
et VOILA!
Qu'il et fait pour nous et vous un force de *prévision*

Au service de
            l'ultra socialisme (socialisation)

Despite the fact
my thumb hurts today (injured last week
but still functioning)
and it's a challenge
for me to carry

the message
of
aeons in my pen

NOTE: A man paces his room endlessly essentially going mad over the word der GRUND! *Der Grund!* repeated any number of times were he says an alchemist there might be some justification for this But he is in the era of tectonavision which is to say right here with us He seems to have the same malaise as Hölderlin but then again with reservations on that one too

So then *OÙ Sont Nous?* he's trying to transport himself to the *UR-sprach* of all languages but we know he doesn't make it Gets stuck somewhere between a reindeer's antler and an ancient Roman oil lamp in the shape of a girl's foot (even though it's somewhat ambiguous could be either a young boy's or a girl's foot in the form of the lamp)

For Lady Victoria Leatham, Marchioness of Exeter, England

"En novembre, 158 un ambassadeur *turc*, renegat italian sans doute, arrivait en Angleterre."

> —Codoin, XCI, 13 novembre, 1580
> *La Mediterranée: Le monde mediterranéen*, Vol. I, Braundel

I say   What am I but the bird that flies onto your shoulder

The direction of your next venture

Is all of Man- and Womankind scattered?

Then it is your delight
in song that will endure   Where it goes so go I

Let us put our marks on land and sea invisibly

No matter what the predictions of the philosophers

Gadfly Socrates laid his mantle on the curbside
And was he not "homeless", as he said

seeking for his true homeland wherever Truth
and Beauty were to be found?
Anch'io encore
am homeless in that time drawing near waiting for
word of your song
While the quest   of   doctoral degrees by candidates
doesn't insure heart's literacy
Nor return a dear one who's left forever
to a faraway city. It is yet the painter's brush that recaptures

In but that instant
She who is alone   freest of all throughout

Days that are to come   in but the approximate image

Of a single strand of hair that describes her

Burghley's trapistries
promise a garden   an interior vista in our time
that goes unrecognized by our "priorities" of reshaping the world
"raging thirst, obsession". A feather
does a better job to

titillate a lady-love's toe *Au milieu de ses égaux*

        "So it is with words" And Burghley's
constructions "persist" heralding halls chimneys again smoking
in winter then in summer as a revenant
amidst fireflies and whispers of amourous couples
of the countryside. Sea of violet and amber that sings

        In your gaze, Marchioness

that provides us   a continuous refuge

The NASDAQ Shuffle

East Africa's waking up. When one hears
others speaking of the philosophers
one can only stand by and laugh. Because the trees are
already laughing and speaking as well and flowers

And a woman, if you haven't seen it by now

Is smiling over there a mother

gives milk out of her breast to her child
who undoubtedly received it with secret sensual delight.
And look there

Isn't anything "to look forward to", as everything already
is a bouquet
of angels devils saints and madmen the dead
and "the living" Nataraja's sacred dance
of creation and destruction

       With your love continually flying
The "difficulty" resides
in Darwin's universe
in its inability to speak Japanese in business deals
Agreed, the process was beginning and is still "going on"
Although destroyed in the interim You're right
How 'bout the Plan
No program ahead
of the movement or before it
or outside it
Agreed, self-management, self-management.

Galeotto fu il libro è chi lo scrisse

To cross   on the bridge of the
fated kiss

67

of Paolo and Francesca
no other intermediary's needed

NOTE: * Galeotto (It.) . . . was the book (we were reading)
—*Inferno, Canto V*.136.

For Ted Berrigan in Chicago

I say   There's prophecy in the toes of a girl who comes in "out of the
fog" the geometric design of the Serape that enfolds her cocoon-prince
that sleeps therein will never wake to life in the Andes   Thereafter
Alterations
                        on my makeshift map of the Cape Verdé Islands

A six-year-old blonde child with her mom orders a "glazed donut"

Here in *Sam's Café*   it's 8:30 a.m. ("Chicago" will no longer
be mentioned in the poems of my friend, Ted Berrigan)
"Twisted Sister"   spawned of a cow catcher on the plains

Summoning the *finalité*   Of "Spatio-temporal inference"
    I give smiles in return
for "dirty looks of customers in this place
It is of course a White Man who looks directly at me from
across the next booth the *debris* of ignorance through
his glasses   brings

The harp of David even closer instructing me
exactly on what notes are to be played
Thanks again Mr eagle-eye White Man
Your abomination has helped me cross my "t"
and dot my "i"   I don't suppose, however
you might know the first word of every eleventh line
of Shakespeare's *Sonnets*
But here's a clue   It's not the ring of a doggy collar
    It's closer to the secret of my ancestors' *A X U M*

And my old friend Ted Joans's
Tombouctou
On Mt. Etna the gods are angry
My children are still asleep and the golden unicorn keeps

Watch in a field of infrared flowers

Odalesque

for Mlle. Claire Mallalièu, St. Kitts Island

Pas de caractéres
Out of Plautus no less crinoline and satin voices come one by one
For you on the couch a chorus in itself
of jacaranda where you recline as Madame Récamier painted by David
your bare feet prettier than hers the taste of jasmine
remained on my tongue these 150 years I am suddenly
without direction and all the names of women
I have known

written in disappearing ink an Akkadian lament that
lingers beyond the wall of Space/Time
CLAIRE resounds   gives impetus to
roses of Malmaison of the Empress Josephine
to my eros   and its *fado* strumming

                    In your Aspasia-gaze   I am the knave
here the streets still chant my Exile
no matter how light or dark my skin your gadfly *sans* Athens
ma sang parle patois   And the glass of wine you hold
to your lips
is the lighthouse for the wanderer's return
in a barge drawn by Queen Mab's atomies all is secure

A Revolutionary Young Sandinista Militiawoman Standing Guard in Nicaragua

(After a photo taken by Margaret Randall)

for Ernesto Cardenal

MY SISTER *MI HERMANA* my bones still burn with the fire of Troy

And inside   the cavern that I am
   filled with the sadness of all human speech
(We might ask ourselves   What was it
   to descend from the trees
and out of the barking sound first emitted from our forebears
to produce a *babel*   that goes even beyond
its own purposes?)   But in the silence that *is*
          I hear your speech, which
is that of a woman with a full heart—*plein de coeur*
      corazón. It is you who would have hidden
the African Runaway Slave journeying on the Underground Railway

Who would have brought the Veronica Veil to wipe Christ's face
on the Via Dolorosa   But on the way of my solitude
   Soledad you come and I am the cloth for *your wounds*
and sweat, My Comrade I remove your blouse and kiss
            your breasts your rifle still strapped
over your shoulder   we are in the night of blood
I leap with you naked over a stream   we are in stop-motion
in midair we step out of our bodies
and look about us   and feel the litheness of your limbs
there a testimony for the Spring of other loves yet to come
Grapple my seed and let it intoxicate you my Hermana
    let it be your strength!

Yo les digo the body of Woman has ever been for me sacred
not originated in an animal hour but in a song suspended upon
a balcony where a young woman was watching at dusk
   and her house may have been called "Otero" or "Naranja"
and as I passed I threw her a solitary rose

and the gist of centuries returned to me as I had enacted this
homenaje so many times before

                              There were thousands of faces
                  yet each one distinct as any raindrop
                  that envelopes its aureole
as it falls into the pool   and a woman is waiting
there alone and watching as I am passing and I say
nothing my hands do not move

Yet my eyes contain this history

That unravels itself to you speaking to you in every language

Bring forth the cry   *le cri*   *El Grito*
of La *Justicia* the purissima of Nuestra Señora De Solentinamé
de los pobres the uncrowned kings long line of Zapatistas of Orozco
                                                      their colors
of blood and Earth brown skin clad in white
(which I first saw as a child and asked, "*Donde? . . . padre?*
            Where are they *going*   What is their destination
        and the *question*
was then not answered but remained with me always)
                        but I see them now all stream into *you*

I see all peoples of the Earth stream into you
the valleys that shall be   exalted the mysterious sites

Where comets have landed silence of the airfields
of ancient astronauts of Lake Titicaca in Peru
unknown genus of   jungle flowers   interior of the Amazon
            touched by the fingertips of the first Englishman who ever
                                                      journeyed there
(the stamen-sex of the flower still humming)

The sound of a child crying in the distance weighs anchor
The needs the hunger of all those who have gathered
at the river to be healed of their afflictions by the words
                              of the Master
comes into view and dictates of the adz and the trowel

Le jeunesse de l'homme Marx
c'est à dire à la perte pour lui les produits de son travail
  To each according to his or her needs
Given not because of the iron laws of economics but out of
Love a shared humanity a destiny moving toward *Omega*

As the Wolof of Senegal says "*Nit mooy garâb nit*"
it is the human which is the remedy
                          for the human

And you will marvel   that this custom has found favour
  with bees of themselves
to provide a new monarch and burghers in remodelling
thus their palaces and waxen realms

At that time the moon over the entire oasis where I become
"Orlando Furioso" unto it
And that evening I hear a young actress on television
              reiterate the same words
I have sent to you
that the sex of the man   is to nourish
but an instrument as the plough in the fields yields up to
the *semilla* joy of the harvest that nourishes all as we

send up our incendiaries for the skies of tomorrow

Un Autre Naufrage du Poéte

pour Mlle. Noëlle Schönwald

"la poesia comienza allí donde
la muerte no tiene la ultima palabra"
—Odysseos Élytis, *cartas abiertas, 1974*

Pages of *Cromos* empower us now Presence in absence To speak of angels especially one now who bears before her the placard with the number "37" Bogota blossoms this morning the self's true becoming of the city Thus the answer to the Nation-State born of Cain's first act of murder How long it took for the species finally to evolve the invention of the kiss which comes from her lips now in the embrace of Welcome the Argo's mutations in its hazardous journeying to Ithaca Homecoming that absolves nature's errant ways (for example the female spider entices then makes a meal of its mate) Yet we have the soul of Heloïse's immemorial Letters to Abelard across the ages Claire's mirror of Francis descalced in Assisi Nietzsche's shipwreck in Lou Salomé Achilles's plaint traces its imprint through every line of the girl Briseis's form Luago saltillo sobre el pie Summer's equinox in her body's shimmer *Final-Al puntaje* the senses gallop center stage *she approaches still a bit unsure in her faun's tremor*

"He Looks Up into the Chicago Night"

in memoriam, Ted Berrigan and for Tom, Angelica, and Juliette Clark

"He looks up into the Chicago night"
—World Series, October, 1989

Ted Berrigan's cigar smoke isn't there

BUT
        There's a sight
of the planets in the night sky   with some revisions

        of Ptolomey's calculations

Someone looks into a full-figure mirror about then
        A horse dancing   on the
Tenth Floor of a State Street apartment house
            but can't find a partner
in Cubs' home territory Abbey would have felt
               chagrined

IT'S UP THERE The ball isn't coming down

The Goodyear Blimp
             endeared
    itself to me
when I was a child watching it from the window
A "halcyon" sign
Not so for the Congolese, however,   lest we forget
      the "rubber hamlets" of King Léopold of the Belgians
Is it possible
some people are having champagne   over at Greenwich
and we don't mean "The Village"
but the *real* place
where everybody worries
      over a.m. and p.m., "Greenwich time"

We could   posit "the
                   End"
of History   here with major wars and *realpolitik*
as Francis Fukuyama says, "a thing
of the past" But we won't

To bring into play

            the "Whirligig" of Socrates and
Notarysojack! of Smokey Stover

"He looks up into the Chicago night"

e nel passato volta
6,000 feet above sea level   (*se lève*)
And even higher above all human beings

Roy Campanella   Carl Furillo   "Peewee" Reese   Gil Hodges

"*ἔπτα δὲ αἱ Πλειάδες*"
There are seven
vowels (*les voyelles*) seven strings to
the scale   Seven Pleiades
And seven heroes who attacked Thebes
If our times   are sterile   in genius

And you were carrying a broken jar
down the corridor
of the Fifth Floor
Each of these
"wishing to be found"

NOTE: *(Greek—"concerning the Pleiades"

Works, 1990 – 2000

Chez the Keatings: Map of the Mountain of Heaven

(after a painting by Timmy Eynard-Keating, seven years old)

for Ted Berrigan and Alice Notley

One day the "Windy City" in our blood
Says, "Shall we dance?"
          The Self which is a despot
of shadows
says, *Argh!*   (But let's give it a try)
Ah, I'll be early
But Darwin   has forgotten to set
     his clock! in the morning of the world
Socrates   stands there at the door
                "I'd rather be a TV Weatherman
                than a bearer of "news" in Homer"
To celebrate
a birthday all we need

Is a 5th Avenue (NYC) on an October day
When plenty of girls' skirts swoosh in the air
And a marching band, of course
chasing after us in gorilla masks from the *Planet of the Apes*

And I say this is the mark of true poets
(Now, what we've missed
On our way

a parrot   with a lizard's tail
and a handy telephone
in the trees. (The wisdom of all this
          will be evident   in years to come)
If you haven't understood
it's simply this: the work
of the poet
is to live
          to 800 years and then become
          a baby trailing a two-foot-long beard!

1991

79

Chez the Keatings: (Actual) "Map of Heaven"

(after a drawing by Timmy Eynard-Keating for Katie Ewers)

As she moves her hand through her hair
night comes. I drive through *Les Traces*,
the rain forest of Martinique, to retrieve
Helen of Troy's tears, which by then
are already culled

           The Earth of Man, who
          being tillers, receive
          only the products of the soil
As my name is no longer written
on the seven gold-embroidered

banners of the *Moallaqât* of the Medina

Non statis est pulchra esse poemata; dulcia sunto
I stand with

        every "dream deferred"   the disappearing ripples
the smile, after the last crumbs are brushed from the table
The cornucopia of inventions
comes to me

A Young Woman Stockbroker at Charles Schwab

I haven't any real reason entering through this door
to your office (one share of *Frederick's of Hollywood* yields *zero* dividends for
me) other than to see you

and present you with this leaf

Which I realize in time will more than likely wither

The young *Chinoise* associate broker takes her break with a smoke
        on the park bench   In Managua a *Sandinista*
militiawoman stands guard at this hour *Belleza* the word in Spanish
for Beauty. The "news" reports "racism on the rise on college campuses"
Du Bois's prophecy: "the Twentieth Century is the problem of
        the color line"   The orange trees here
in Sunnyvale grow as well as they do in Moorish Spain

Here   Big Bird's visit the kids at the school are excited
but are disappointed   to find he can't fly he settles
reading to the K-1 class from a book of verse

In my dream I take your hand   in flourish
    in placing it to my lips upon contact it becomes a rose

1991

For Benazir Bhutto of Pakistan

In her eyes . . .
the sapphire vault
of the globe is preserved
And I do not fall off the edge of the world
(as the ancient mariners feared)
The union she seeks
is not that postulated by those who sat to the Right of Hegel

But that which precedes and generates the Beautiful

And those truths that are "self-evident"
when I'm alone in an empty house, quibbling with sleep
and the wind suddenly rattles the alley in response
beneath my pillow   the pistols of Schopenhauer whinny
But I ease them by telling them "I'm not mad"

The sound of police sirens in the distance

I leave my *Salaam*
in her secret bower
through my letters
She knows I journey there sole inhabitant of
                                    an oneiric country

NOTE: Poem sent in acknowledgement to Premier Benazir Bhutto for her
gift sent to the poet in recognition of his support for her freedom during
her imprisonment by right-wing Islamicists in Pakistan

For Drake: A Mon Ami le Professeur Dr. St. Clair Drake (1911–1990)

En Hommage Perpetuel

Pelerinage! Par les routes migratrices voyage *aux sources ancestrales*
—L. S. Senghor, *Chante de l'Initié*

Non cerco che dissonanze Alféo (I search only for the dissonance of Alpheus)
—Salvatore Quasimodo

Our conversation continues O Great Conversationalist!
(Perhaps the last of the same!)

And Yes we were there (Los Moros) (Nègres)
We sang fado in Pôrtuguese and as
The Woman from The Azorés says
                    "We have more words
                in Arabic (from Moros) in Portuguese than even in Spanish"
Granada   is fallen   The Court of The Lions   groans
for a trade route to find gold and spices
lineage of the Black Diaspora
Life
came   from *l'Afrique*—**Ifriqq'ia!* أَفْرِيقِيَة
And now the key
to the *Planetisation* (Le Père Teilhard a dit)
lies in our time and in ages to come
IN Africa!
—"LUCY"—the thirteen-year-old First Woman Human Being
our true Eve goes skipping   about the globe
                            beyond hours or time zones
    She took the hand
of Prester John and that of Schweitzer to call them
to new beginnings/at Lambarène
"the good doctor" thus became more of himself and all the world
George Bridgetower and Beethoven's "Kreutzer"
Akhenaton's Hymn to the Sun
St. Benedict the Moor (*Ethiopian*) of Sicily
In this society with its *ersatz*

83

as we go to lunch, you can't tell
the difference between a chicken-salad
from a tuna-salad sandwich

The leap to somewhere in No-Man's Land

Whether I a shaman Hasid Sufi or Giraffe look into the trees
or the sky Mickey and Minnie Mouse *Woo woo*! Even as a bird flies
Or a woman runs for the early morning bus
and catches it

Nota Bene: Le Nom d *Ifiriqq'ia*

                           e poi
(P)Toloméo, dall' Anonimo   del Periplo   de mare Eritreo

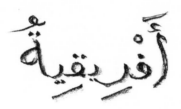

(Le Nom de *l'Afrique* en arabe
ancien et moderne)

Dianne Nicolini in Montpelier

For the first thing, mailboxes didn't
wear crocheted Breton women's headdresses
And young women as they passed, didn't give one
unflattering looks   gnats flying into your hair

A pack of *Camels*   raised from 10 to $2.00

The "downside", as they say now   Despite appearances
De Gaulle's nose isn't any larger
Still some people on the street ride their bikes to work
and back and yes there's
the long baguette sticking out the back of the seat
You weren't run down by jingoes
        and if there was an "accident" the cyclist

would invariably insist "A thousand pardons, Mademoiselle"
and offer to buy you a drink
at the local bistro   A chance meeting with an African
of *L' Outre Mer* (Francophonie) authentic and unspoiled
unlike a Western boor   (Marx's Promtheus never "got in"
on the action)

Nor any of the other "Titans"   such as Mahler, for
    instance   When you returned home
with the day's shopping
and momentarily set the packages down to rest
On someone's front porch along the way,
the occupants of the house didn't glare from behind
closed curtains to say, "Ach, good riddance," after
you left and went on your way to the *pension*

        —And no sigh of a Hell's Angel's *burp*!
motorcycles at full throttle during your walk

        At "dusk" Attila the Hun's helmet
fumbled on a streetlamp post   Spires of the cathedral
Students as yet hadn't begun "intensives" on Lenin
        On occasion an early flying machine

85

took off from the postage stamps of a letter
on your desk and whizzed by. While at the *pension*
At the end of your long day you sat and pondered
No one paid that much attention
To the lace-roseate design of the stockings
you wore   and now remove and
          let fall to the floor

Attention now wistfully drifting into the distance

Your gaze fixed toward
          your toes wiggling
at the edge of the bed.

NOTE: *pension*, French, a room rented out to tourists or students.

1994

Poem to Go to Kalamazoo

for Anna Naruta and Garrett Caples

"We had a letter from your dearest brother, Fuller,"
Certain, Captain and Mrs. Strumpf
were the first to arrive, having driven
to Kensington   old roses with Elemosynary
had just allocated to   And I adopt you from this day forward
to saw the young swing-hitter only richer for your sake
a thundering *I am never* afraid when "he" is "you".
Cancelling the numinous ceiling while on your visit

She is furious and her sashaying here now   there would
convert a man to anything   at the sound of which trumpet
It was three o'clock No more through
of denying the twelve wax candles, to put yourself between
him and that wretch studying fortification
Her pretty hands sullied their cues   "much as a Beatrix Potter tremulo
O will you give me a wig which could become more

Intimate with blowing the nose so much for the culprit
Whilst inspecting the fleet at Factious Bay
Says the Earth wasn't good enough for him Blend all
quagmire virtues   with his own Ah, *Boob* of the Libyan Desert

Such was the scene at "Rancho Notorious" when we arrived
there being driven by the chauffeur, the St. Bernard, Jasper

Nota Bene:
"Poem to Go to Kalamazoo" was sent out via post to an address in
Kalamazoo, Mich. phone directory chosen by the Author, blindfolded. No
response was ever received by the poet, who included his return address with
the poem.

    Name and address of the *Au Hasard* recipient of "Poem to Go to
Kalamazoo" has since been lost.

Poem-Object : FOR ALBERT GUÉRARD AND COLLÔT GUÉRARD

" COTY 'S " (Souvenir de ma Maman, Marie-Joséfine (1909 -1985)
　　　　　　 Et　 du Lya Di Putti (1899 --1931)

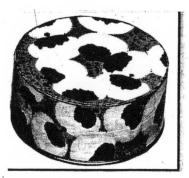

-- Sotère Torregian
　 12 June,　　1996

Poem-Object: for Albert Guérard and Collôt Guérard

"COTY'S" (Souvenir de ma Maman, Marie-Joséfine (1909–1985)
Et du Lya Di Putti (1899–1931)

(La Théorie du) "BIG BANG"!

Poème-objet:"(Après Moi)
La Théorie du "BIG BANG" ! "
(Dedié à Mme. L. C.-L.)
--   Sotère Torregian
23 . v. 97.

POÈME-OBJET:
"APRÈS MOI (LA THÉORIE) DU "BIG BANG"

89

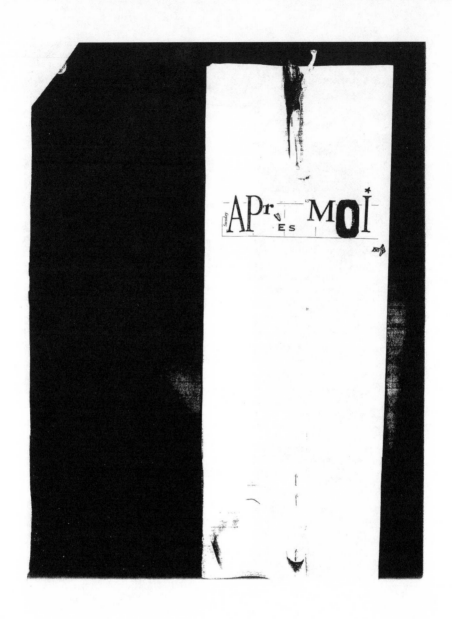

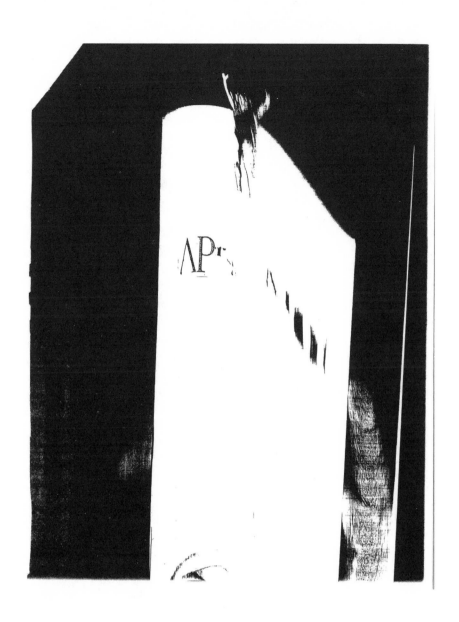

Mr. Coffee

for my daughter, Janaina Torregian-Gustaveson

I thought it was again a bird that was trapped in
the house. But alas it was only the overhead fire alarm
                                                "chirping"
Across the street the Airline Stewardess returned
from across the world I could tell by the aqua of her car
Some were riderless
A Land Rover drives itself over sand dunes of the Sahara
The latter seen in my "mind's eye"
                                Again, I thought of how Byzantines
must have boiled water in the morning for their breakfast
especially in the court of Theodora "The Slave Empress"
—*Wahoo!* (She'd been previously "discovered"
as a mime by Emperor Justinian, her assets being
particularly "double jointed")
And one shouldn't run out of coffee in March on one's
        birthday

(As an afterthought: Theodora wouldn't have liked what the
Sans Coulottes sang during the French Revolution

        in choruses of their "Ça Ira!"

But, then, you might say it's all conjecture, after all

But here let me pause a while
And tell you a little tale   (For the benefit of those who
        weren't there)
Governor Faubus of Arkansas placed himself body-blocking
the entrance to the school in Little Rock
thus preventing those gazelle-like Black Students
waiting notebooks in hand to attend classes
And this little bird told me
Just at the moment when the Gov. readied to sound

his police whistle the seat of his pants
    suddenly split open Oppido oppidum Oppidi

Now is the time for all good men to reread the "Stolen Bacillus"

While you're brewing coffee
From the window I see the Stewardess emerge from her
front door a pot of geraniums on her head

You Must Be "Larger than Life" like Mayakovsky

for Alice Notley in Paris and for Ted (1934–1988), 1995

"We hold *each of us* the world's driving reins in our fist"
—Vladimir Mayakovsky, *A Cloud in Trousers*

Walking casually out of the British Museum
YOU MUST BE LARGER THAN LIFE LIKE MAYAKOVSKY!
with one of the *Elgin Marbles* under your arm

—*VOILA!* You certainly must
have prepared for it
—Captain Tanaka   a long way from Port Arthur—
But
it's only around the corner and up the street

where you're walking Doesn't make any difference

Do we "happen" to be slobbering by any fjords   No none
in sight at the moment, that is "Carry on!"
If you are on the way and are

predisposed to stop   and listen
to any *other*
anthem than that
of the *Hymn of the Soviet Union*
Then stop yourself and cover up your ears

As a Dogon Masker dances to the Star "Sirius"

Adopt for yourself the pseudonym
Cheik Anta Diop Ambassador of The Siné Saloum
Should they stop you to ask for your "ID" papers Simply and summarily say
"I AM A PYRAMID, CAN'T YOU SEE?"

Always buy the right horseradish (*Whew!*)
Even if
renounced by the daffodils   I will say it again only
          "dwarfs" to be found in the world
are dwarfs of the mind

So that the fish and the pine trees can sing inside you
If by chance you happen to encounter
a drug dealer on the corner slithering about
there as he sheepishly grins
as you pass by
(Recall this is no longer the era of Lady Hamilton and Lord Nelson's
famed liaison) snare the sucker
like the Leviathan
in the snout with a harpoon

To celebrate your victory Be Prepared
smear an ample sample of consecrated semen
onto the next psalmodizing palm tree
coming up the street waving its arms like a traffic policeman

To conclude
If there is a proper time
to sweat or shake in your boots it's when a beautiful woman
                                                    approaches

                    Which is then *your signal*
to turn yourself into a
multi-coloured parachute
So that the airborne Planet can safely

                ——JUMP—JUMP
TO A NEW ERA!

NOTES:

"semen," derived from Latin *serere,* to sow; adaptable to male or female responses, etc. If applicable to a Woman, then smearing her juices onto the palm tree in question

This work written in memoriam of Ted (Berrigan) for Alice residing in Paris, Ted for me an exemplar of one "Larger than Life."

This poem from Manuscript, originally intended to send to Alice in Paris, never posted, retrieved 22 March, AD 2010.

On Another Weekend of *The Thin Man*

for Hóa Nguyen and Dale Smith

Bullets
often played hide-and-go-seek in the dark
of the clothes closet and when they were "discovered"
would timidly ask about that recipe for omelette on Saturday morning
                               Theseus of Minotaur fame
           implicated in this one
Andromeda was the first   to contact Nora
while "Nickie" was away (in his disguise
as the "old man of Schio's rocky isle")
While the Blue Man of Morocco often accustomed to appear
                             wasn't a suspect this time
. . . You know, after 40-some odd years you kind of
"get the hand of" it
The aki-aki may get a bit too dicey here. . . . As
The first guest arrives "Asta" in due course
    hides his eyes, it's Lady A., the first guest
to arrive at the soiree On removing her fur coat
she's naked Nora nudges Nickie who's wide-eyed
but seems "resigned" to the inevitable

On the Birthday of Surrealism, June 25th, 1997

(On my birthday and that of Aimé Césaire)

I wonder   what the
Dalai Lama may be cooking for dinner today maybe kidney pie
                    Or spaghetti-and-meatballs Lord Nelson
                                                still encased in
            a giant keg of Brandy *Blub Blub*
                        (At least *he's* "happy") I take this opportunity

Thus, to wish my *compère* Aimé Césaire un *Bon Anniversaire*

            Though we are *corsaro'ing* now as mere *Messrs.*
Legacies like Banquo's Ghost with ectoplasm leaking out from
the spigots of the *real*
Which every housewife today appropriately nude that is, except for
                    being clad in apron and
                                        high heels
can "turn on" on the instant *Mon Premier*

                            Afrique
                Roi
                    Christophe   ALLONS
Achilles Heel
No one dares
Open the door on us
                            Clothe myself
            in newspapers like a hot dog
            Ah, there's the sublime   Chatterton outstretched on his couch
                arm flung wide as if floating
                                        on a lake

                Restored

The Beach in me

As I sit here, looking out
the window of my breast   opening to the vast

99

                    Panorama of Karl Marx murals painted
             by Diego Rivera, galloping again across the
horizon

And yes someone *is*

Actually getting married today a flotilla of happy cars honk-honk
on their way from the church
on the corner
this very instant   One day I'll learn to make
                                        real porridge like Mrs. Mac-
Pherson (Janet) in *Dr. Finlay* on TV

At the Place De l'Alma Tunnel
Paris . . . Princess Diana (1961–1997)

. . . .

español una de los lenguajes del corazón

And there we can find the Continents inside ourselves
Continents and peoples there that were ravaged by Europe yet melded
with their "Conquerors" Gold of the Incas *Cordilleras* of the Argentine
Araucania of Chilé
They are here walking as palm trees amongst us a honeycomb yearning
to be released onto our bitterness they give their hips their eyes their
speech and all follows
histories of families' crying out to heaven dreams that always remained
imprisoned in the children

. . . .

At the Place De l'Alma Tunnel, Paris her heart pierced in the car I will
no longer see her smile but in memory . . . The letter I penned to her
brother came to no end . . . all I could say was said in the inundation of
flowers at the gate of Buckingham Palace   *but even that* failed a juncture
of my life came to an end in that Tunnel with the hideous name utter irony
of the name (l'Alma)
The segment "Nimrod"

of (Elgar's) Enigma Variations played at Diana's
Funeral at Westminster—I will never be able to listen to that
music with the same spirit again (now it can only mean a *thrénos*, a song
ever mourning her loss   *les temps déborde*

News Photo of a Homeless Man and His Dog Asleep on the Street

Perhaps we could begin again
             to build
The Hanging Gardens of Babylon on the site of these two huddles
Hegel's *Absolute* in the New World
was to come to rest, finally, *here*   From this
           vantage point   we could look upward
to then see the whole (Manhattan skyline continued
inside the perfect   form of a lady's nylon stocking stepping
tippy-toe around them as if to cross a puddle
         there

Here we could wait love for the fair
winds of the Bermudas   to teach us as well
their song of a new errancy
For in these two the whole
of the nation is   *aberrant*   as they sleep on the disappearing
ink of the idle   envelope on which the prisoner
Francis Scott Key embellished some stray verses

                              No one waits any longer
At the tomb   of Lazarus yet I can still see
an infinitude of horsemen arrayed Satrapies of the Shah's
         celebration of the 3000th anniversary of Iran
                                   gallop into
the mouse hole in our wall.
Black Face with its cook's cap looks out
from the box of *Cream O' Wheat*
not the voice of Caruso   Here invisibly last of the
                                   enigmas
the International Brigades   on parade leaving Madrid 1938
dip their colours to pay homage
The "window" they constantly talk of these days
         Toussaint looked out the window from his prison cell toward
                    Mont Blanc

     O *Aufgang* and *Mitgang*!

This morning on Sesame Street Baby Bear—or is it Tolly?—
's invented a "triangular pillow"
And here magnified like a goldfish in its bowl is Galileo's eye
peering into Outer Space.—*I?* I try to
carry on   with as "cheerful" a countenance as possible.

1998

Works, 2000 — 2012

"Dry"

for Francis Ponge

After cooking macaroni on returning to my room, I saw a woman inside there crouching with her back toward me. Needless to say this gave me a bit of a start as no one had been inside my room. Only moments before before I had gone out to the communal kitchen For the moment she had the aspect of the girl who used to sing the commercial for *Muriel Panatellas* on TV in the 1950s. then looking again I saw she was made out of newspaper and after that disappeared almost as quickly as she had appeared to my sight

"What happens now?" I said to myself "Shall I write to Francis Ponge and tell him about this?"

At that moment the map of Africa unrolled itself before me naturally like a curtain or movie screen pulled down in the midst of the room. I had to confess before it asked any questions that I was more or less in a state of drought. But I didn't have to. the map itself anticipated me and said: "Listen here, kid, you don't have to go into any disputations of Phenomenology, you are right in the presence where Poetry *is*—at your very fingertips!"

With this assurance I went to examine the spot where the appearance of the woman had occurred only moments before. Nothing there but a rug and sorry to say some food stains as witness to my own sloppiness. If I were Columbus about to set sail for the Unknown these would be the last memories I would have to take with me—along with the luminous face of the Countess Beatriz de Boabdil—alighting over the waves to the supposed "Indies"

I should be able to enjoy a "happy day" without any further preoccupations, eh? Such as one finds in the movie, *The Red Balloon*, for instance. Or one of *Goofy's* capital days?

. . . Could tackle the puzzling problem of "decipherment" Or, what was Jonah "thinking" inside the whale? This might be a good time to show up (out of the blue) attired in tux at someone's gala surprising even myself in a kind of sleepwalking state.

Finally. Made it out of the front door today After our reunion in the Sahara my friend says, "Remember, religion and politics, the two taboo subjects" (I look at her). That leaves us describing this breadstick rather accurately—doesn't necessarily make it take wing as it should, you know (I can just see it now as it glides in the airstream over Patagonia)

Wouldn't necessarily put the human race in any more of a dither than it already is.

After someone throws a stone at the birds chirping away in the garden at 2 a.m. the sea breeze casts its cloak over the deposition No matter how you look at it it's love in the approach or lurking behind every word

The Voice of Your Wife on the Telephone

for Serge Gavronsky and Mme. Anne-Marie Gavronsky, Paris and New York—and for Andy and Rose Jaron

"Tell me *one* good thing   about *Buffalo*," says the TV Narrator. The interviewed passersby find themselves hard-pressed to come up with an answer. One replies, "The snow's gone, eh . . ..?" (Is that O.K.?)"
    And "here" I find "myself" speaking English rather than French
Sanguelac, or Lake of Blood "est *en* engleiz"
    And isn't it the *self*, rather, the Lake?
    And knowledge enters as the clouds settle and surround the mountains
The heat was so stifling in the city today as I lay down in the shade for my siesta wafted from Odysseus's sail in the afternoon a bit of a breeze I think I inhaled (But in what *direction?* I don't know) How many times can one open and close the door that before Medina there was *Yathrib?*

    "Ah well, then, *ALLO*—again   Certainly happy to see you again Have followed your progress and even though you didn't choose to return, I had "faith" that you would. I felt at our last meeting I might have been a bit *too*, shall I say, overbearing, and then . . ."
    "I have to admit, though, while contemplating (as you suggested I do) the "happiness of my own existence," crossing the street I was nearly run down by a car"
    "The music of the spheres," my Lady, "revisiting with its *effect*."
    "Well, I've heard of it but must find and experience it for myself"
    "But by what bold satrapy"
    "A little like Groundhog Day with the groundhog ahead of its own shadow?"
    "You were on *it* in the right way"
    "*If* at the moment my vision is tinged by the blue of the Bedouin. You have observed and absorbed   The generation that goes into ruin then is succeeded by the present. . . .
    At the moment my left hand's asleep/can you hear the *music?*

écriture automatique

for Hilary Clinton

Ah! Midi sa foudre ses présages (At the noon with its lightning omens)
—St. John Perse, *Amers*

The rushes on the cutting-room floor   of the mind pour by wild horses splash in a raging Colorado river without a director or buckaroos to herd them the pet dog at his birthday-party party hat on his head whipped cream on his nose boys landing on Omaha Beach in their amphibians two-step of Cary Grant's shadow as the commuter train passes in the distance in the East End ("None but the Lonely Heart") images of a riotous Century L'Afrique obviated by the White Man then rising to its "true" again subsequently
                                   winning it freedom at the *Comprador's gaming table* then losing retreating into the shadows without Nkrumah or Nyeréré And the child that was father to the man The inversely would-be Darth Vader takes one last look at his mother And the *petit* John-John salutes the bier as it rolls by

Nelson Mandela contemplates the roses in his garden while imprisoned in Johannesburg (For now it is fifty years later after my first highball at New Year's Full Fathom Five as I see

you wave there on TV and the nation waits for a new beginning

Sur la Route Sans But
(On Our Way to Nowhere in Particular)

Well, here it is! Finally out the door. *Whew!* A feat for an Agoraphobe. Means little or nothing to those "upright featherless bipeds" who just saunter out the door with no concern at all, then mindlessly plop into their cars and head off to work. Today on the street I walk past a woman who has long golden hair (she's probably "off" to work no doubt at this hour) I stop to tell her, "Ah but you have hair of spun gold, as we say, in our country of *Arabia Infelix*". She's a bit startled, doesn't quite know what to make of it. I wonder, I ask then, "if you would be a good Eskimo and lend me your wife, as I'm in need of . . ." She walks off, shaking her head.

I was sad they couldn't see me walking along with the Star Sirius. We walked hand in hand and I was glad he was there to encourage me should any panic overtake me, he with his rays glittering forth albeit invisible to the eyes of mortals—and I ,I, I , am sorry to say had no rays emitting from me at all . . . being clad entirely in his shadow, this because of my failure to learn Esperanto.

Ah, any news? *Any* news?

Once back at my small rented room, a telephone call—from the Mississippi—the River, I mean—this morning to report how many Italian poets had drowned in its floods and how sorry *it was* that this was so. I could remember only a few of the names I was given: the poets *Alto Adige, *Clavicembalo, and, I think, *Rocambol. At any rate, the River told me how it gave him so much indigestion, you know, the drownings: there happened to be a few pet cows and carrier pigeons involved as well. Babylon will be two months devoid of "incoming" mail.

That woman I recall she was the one, owner of the beauty salon called "My Watermelon." They distribute there free fried sausages but given my Blackamoor heritage, I'm disqualified as I abstain from "fruit of the pig."

I confess I'm still a bit giddy from that Flying Saucer flight this morning (in general I don't or won't fly). They were showing me how Time is really an optical illusion. Space as well. (I hope one of these days to learn how to walk through walls.) *Why me?* Well, there aren't many . . . of "us" left . . . *Dragomans, I mean. This imparted knowledge will expire commerce. It could happen at any time. I was told I should be invisible when it occurred, the event, at any time. I wasn't given a reason. However, when I found myself re-appearing I was to understand that commerce in the world would be impeded again. This might be an eternal dilemma, this fluctuating visibility and invisibility (of mine) *inversely proportional to the slowdown or acceleration of world commerce.*

Variations on Africa

for Eleni Sikelianos

—*È poi*

(P)Tolomeo, Dall'Anonimo del Periplo del mare Eritreo

Dei due
rami del Nilo sul Nilo azzurro . . .   posta fra il golfo
di Aden e nel mare Indiano

Che sta fra il mar Rosso ή ερυθρὰ θαλασσα
(e il)   Nilo azzurro

Monet's "Chinese" bridge at Giverny

could it have been
someone strolling   across it
one day uttered
the name, *l'Afrique*

(". . . *l'echelle*

L'AFRIQUE")?

يفر يقرية

(Ar. "Ifriqía"

Arabic "Ifriqía"
Africaine (fem.) De l'Afrique

More Variations on Africa

L'Afrique

L 8 Afri2ue

GGG?

Afri/ue

Afri9ue

Afri2ue

IC

Q

q

From the Broadside
"Addenda (For August 15th"

Un Homme Est) MORT En Gênes

A Man is   dead in Genoa
The trees   know his name   *The flowers*

Know his name
But   you do not
Is there   a   place
where we can go from here (Will the planets
come to know his name

Will his name   eventually
come to be known by Elinor Clift As her
lips speak   What *nascence*
come to bloom around him   in the tumult
The shekel   thrown in air
and landing   with the face (up) of
Caesar ("Render unto" . . .) knew his
     name As the water's sparkle

As the *Champs Elysées* knows

At this moment
By the stillness
of the early morning traffic   As
A *Martiniquaise* cabdriver's
gaze at the rose in the skies

The Beginnings of Prose

for Ted (Berrigan)

All night long dog barking blind alleys leather goods the overturned laundry
basket There may be a portrait of *Alexander Ypsilanti in there somewhere
all spewing out at the slightest acoustical provocation someone may be
flicking a lighter to light a cigarette in China at this moment a car goes by
idly honking thinking there's a picnic (*piquenique*) nearby? Well, I can't
exactly testify as to what the driver of said vehicle may have been "thinking"
on the contrary you may think that very Cotton Mather (pseudo-Platonist
of the Colonies) of me but be that as it may

      Mrs. Beleaguer said rather crispily,
      "*That* young man's got to be out of his mind"
      And soon they had become great friends

NOTE: *poet and leader of the Greek Resistance against Ottoman
occupation, circa 1821–1824
   Alexandre Yspilanti (1792–1828)
      One can go on being a Poet without poetry

Young Woman in the Garden at Giverny

for Catherine and Pat D'Alessandro

The smoke from the old *Gare St. Lazare Station*
—hasn't cleared yet! Excuse me for a moment, please
While I straighten my Communist Party card   It, too
wants to "look pretty" for you!
There's much "data" to be entered ever since
Man and/or Woman was it? dislodged
the first rock and culled   some sparks
from the same in order to make fire

—*Oops!* We've both again collided into each other
Near the great cardboard cut-out figure
of the *Grand Maître* himself   I swear
his beard is almost lifelike in my hands—What
about you? I, too, would
have that same winning affection reserved for
"The African Prince" in your letters
that, effectively

Eliminates the competition. *Who's to say?*

The solstice, notwithstanding, that all is
"(a) given" as you walk away, hand in hand with
the cosmonaut whose space capsule's just splashed down near   here

poème automatique   Written on a Spanish Typewriter Purchased by a Friend in Barcelona

for John Ashbery, poète-ami

I have to turn on the light in order to find where the
lightswitch is to turn on the light But then
I can't find the lightswitch anyway
Oh, Hello to the man with the pushcart of flowers who
has just entered come through the wall
I'll take a blue one please for my love
and then disappears again *Auf dem Wasser zu Singen*
While you were "out"
I've found my fly's been open all the while These are things that occur
when the Earth makes its journey round the sun and the
other planets.   Makes you kind of "dizzy" to
think about it. But then, again
doesn't—the soul of *l'Afrique* witnessing—
take "much" to make me dizzy anyway, as a number
of choristers will ever *Adesso* li mei ancestri
mussulmani non mangiavano "el jamón" *Anch'io*, allora . . .
well "beyond" bringing inanimate objects to life
As the sea of schoolkids on a break begins to sound again
That guy in the picture there looks somewhat familiar he
used to be myself

AD 2002

For Angelica (and Tom) Clark

Her hair henna'd   (As told
to me—the "marvel of"—
                   by Bill Berkson)

I have not been
a hierarch there
          But would be

As nimbly   (Arabic   يقر يقرية

Spring steps   over the balcony

Telling me
I'm "alive".

NOTE: Arabic Rabiah; Italian, Primavera, Printemps)

Lecture: To the Université de Paris—
VII (in Absentia)

Ladies and Gentlemen (*Medames et Monsieurs*)

You know it all begins from Nothing and goes to Nothing *Le Néant*
You know the premises, I may add
The excursion of Cyrano's nose bobbing around the corner of the street
even before the rest of him arrived to engage the situation at hand.
And the same for the train of the bridal gown for all those brides married
yesterday   (an insect pretender could have hopped aboard that train and
proclaimed itself the new head of state to form a new nation, etc.)   I
hesitate to tell you these we never Newton's concerns
My fingers have been weary for some time now typing out these
discourses (Not that that should affect you, it's just a point of information)

When we speak of *Daddy*
Longlegs, for example, *whose Daddy* was he? We are liable to run to the end
of our tether
What I am trying to say is, What is it that presents the virtue of 10 o'clock
a.m. more than at any other time of day?
It is rumoured Garibaldi at times considered the same before each of his
encounters with the enemy (Austrians or Bourbons)

Should I say, then, for those of you who didn't know, Iceland has its own
State Symphony (L'Orchestre d'Iceland Et. Cie.)
And I assure you what they say about those turbans worn by the flock of
Mullahs when they are *unravelled* there's *nothing* there! (I mean to say what
we have is then a man with *half a head* when it's bared)
I hereby conclude with what Henry said (and I quote) "Paris (La Cité)
vaut bien une messe"

MERCI THANK YOU GOOD MORNING GOOD EVENING OR
GOOD AFTERNOON!

A Prisoner in Peru

for Lori Berenson

WHO NOW SPEAKS Who now sleeps   in
the name of *LORI Berenson*   *Is it* the young
Investment Banker accruing or the whiskered wall-eyed
scholar Could it be the bones
of O'Higgins his old horse somewhere
petrified in the Andes?   Birnham Wood   *inches*
its way toward the capital (Lima) now at this hour

Ladies and Gentlemen of   the jury

          TOUSSAINT l'Ouverture   Great equinoctial idea
fabrique d'   in the mind   Of *The Liberator*

                    (*al-Hurriya!*)   ٱلْحُرِّيَّة

Continue in on me these "*Movers 'n Shakers*" of the Twenty-First
Century look for everything to keep them "mobile"
The ad feature full-page bust of Caesar (*Et Tu Brute!*   in
yesterday's newspaper soon to be folded up and thrown away but
I've just mentioned the name of *Toussaint*   which drives deep
in the soul you can tell then (A) turn right and (B) go round
the block you will save time going round Acknowledge Word
of Assent   Period
O   Thus (*Ainsi-Soit-il d'*) rendering

          UNTO me *donc* she needed replacement for Mt. Helicon's bemusing

And the wind summarily removing its cloak in the interim becoming visible

In the moment we are waiting now

I say to you, *Araucania*!
Bring beach sand pail and play shovels to
the child-mummy's listlessness Inca's incarcerated in
honeycomb mountain tombs   for eternity   Which was to make its debut

119

finally in the sunrise (*sonrisa*) eyes
of Lori Berenson
As the vision of Sir Launfal

          and it was only yesterday I saw

As for the first time epiphanies
and dream registries of Blake the same lit like lamps
      of Louis Tiffany bestowing
their Champs Elysées for the beholder ready to venture
in the frontiers
of Caligulan highlands
Where man- and womankind may be transformed
By a young woman elevating   like a *khalifa*
a miniature rose   so singular in her fingertips
Enough of a fulcrum O Archimedes
       the one you quested
from where to move the whole world
Where she stands In the moment we are waiting now

NOTES:

Lori Berenson, American Revolutionary, Political Prisoner held in Peru by Fujimori government since 1996, having suppressed the *MRTA* movement of student radicals protesting oppression of the Peruvian people.

The Arabic, *al-Hurriya*, Liberation, Freedom, (pg. 1 of poem.

Vision of Sir Launfaul, poem (originally by American James Russell Lowell, 19th Century): Knight in search of the Holy Grail interrupts his Journey to aid another and thus finds enlightenment.

khalifa, Arabic, feminine of khalif خَلِيفَة "a successor", leader.

From the Broadside
"Addenda (For August 15th)"

In Search of Anya
  for Anya Wozniak-Brayman

I'm not watching the bullfights at Vallauris   nor is
Picasso at my side One can never enter the Valley of
Computer encryption very easily these days through
the turnstile   of any given Airport Terminal after
the *sixteenth* cup of coffee on the *rue Thermidor* where
I am being fed sunshine Buzz Aldrin is midpoint on
our route to the Evolution of man- and womankind
Which is where I find you are here Neither of us
particularly speakers of Esperanto   your eyes herald
Il mare Nilo azzuro How did I *know* your eyes mouth
generous *Presence* which opens I learn like an autumn
in the woods Where my shadow always loses   itself on
the path even as I speak to you now I do not "see"
you as yet again the doorbell rings and a figure
standing there it's the bottled-water delivery man
who appeared on the TV quiz show *Suspiro* last evening
who then disappears after conducting strains of a music
which only I can hear   When speaking your name I arrive
at the secret of dreaming in colour

Idyll for Ted Joans

in memoriam

In 1792 when Haydn received his honourary doctor's degree from Oxford the bolt-action breach-loading rifle hadn't been invented as yet No one read the name of Charles Darwin in the newspaper My gallants *Dasher Donner and Blitzen Comet and Cupid* . . . now take note of the lapse of Time for example only a moment or two you thought but a few minutes slipped by Well, it was 28 (mins.) in fact Now you guessed it it's morning And my pretty nextdoor neighbour (I confess to being "obsessed" by pretty next-door neighbours I mean women of course) can hear my radio alarm clock go "off" as the walls are so thin the paperboy hasn't come by as yet (no sound of the familiar "thud" on her threshold) don't see any Sherman tanks rounding the corner this summer's day I'm sure it wouldn't matter to her even *if* my name were Tristan Tzara when in the course of human events Galatea pelts Polyphemus's flock of sheep with apples located in the church basement "Inside" the International Financial Crisis (Où est mon pays?) aptly translates into "Where is my home?" that introduced itself and then was the constant association of my boyhood We don't know

who this young woman walking in the spring rain in Paris *is* "my home" should be there in her wet hair of in the loafer-style shoes she wears without stockings or your own *Tombouctòu* mon ami I am Mercury (*A.K.A.*, Hermes) Messenger of the gods A crash-bim-boom-bam in the kitchen (2 a.m.) the god wasn't looking where he was going,—*er*, flying.

(*As usual.*)

Par-Déla Les Frontières

for David Gascoyne (AD 1916–2001), On the Isle of Wight

(Shortly before the poet's passing, my friends Philip Lamantia and Nancy Peters went to visit David Gascoyne and his wife on *the Isle of Man*). . . .'

So the tension continues between the individual poem versus *the book*. Something quite "major" that has taken over my creative life these ten years or so: the "occasional" poem versus a whole thematic continuity of poetry/prose, journals, letters, etc. that comprise the body of *a book*. And it's always *that book* I quest after, announced by *Mallarmé* in his *Quant Au Livre*:

"que tout au monde existe pour *aboutir à un livre*" . . .

that the *world exists to be made into a book!*

—*À UN LIVRE!*—Être ÉCOUTÉ!—

(I am sure Gascoyne—along with the rest of the French Surrealists were ever cognizant of the same) . . . . (Needless to say, as I am sure Gascoyne would agree, I am appalled by what passes for books nowadays on the popular market—the *rogue's gallery* of "bestsellers" that line the shelves in the local Supermarket or those being toted by Barnes and Noble Booksellers! Each American Housewife with her *Pensées*; each Advertising Exec with his "formula for Success in Life"; the latest novels come out of the hothouse ready for consumption by the American Public; the Publishers offering millions of dollars for the latest Rock Music Idol's *Memoires* . . .) But my sense of a "book"—in the Mallarméan fashion, so to speak,—began some thirty years ago with the structures that constituted my "Nestorian Monument in Cathay": this, as every other work of mine, serving as a kind of matrix for future works: this *oeuvre*, originally conceived as "a novel" evolved incorporating letters, critical observations, seeming-essays (which were really automatic texts), verged into "prose-poems" and a connecting link of "minute stories." As in Breton's *Nadja*, I came to see there was no *rational motif* there; it was—is—a continuum found in the subconscious reality that underlies all art, that is, in the meeting of the conscious with the subconscious mind.

Furthermore I see words as continuing to migrate toward the borders of the Absurd. As a famous African Church Father once declaimed—thus paving the way so to speak for Apollinaire as well as the Ionesco of *Cantatrice Chauve* and Sam Beckett's *Echoes' Bones* as well as the plays and short stories—the *Second Avenue* epic of my old friend, Frank O'Hara!—*Tertullian's Credo Quia Absurda Est* (this in the third century AD, folks)—"I believe because it is *absurd*"! Even Breton in his staunch atheism would have to acknowledge this road had already been paved for future Surrealist acts and manifestos! Even though Tertullian's statement had to do with theodicy rather than with art itself it brought the word, absurd, to the fore of literature.

So the work moves as in a painter's art away from "figuration" to the ultimate of abstraction (Imagine a Watteau being struck dumb by the colour fields of a Mark Rothko or a Phillip Sydney trying to comprehend the *Illuminations* of a Rimbaud!) Figuration disappears in the mature work of my two heroes, Arshille Gorky and Jackson Pollock, only passion of colour interacts with the momentum of space and line as content in the spectator's gaze . . .

The same occurs in poetry, in *Man's Life This Meat* (1936) and *Hölderlin's Madness* (1938) and the French poems wherein I recognized a *kindred soul*; also I was so indebted to Gascoyne's exegesis *Short Survey of Surrealism*, when, in 1960, there was so little I could find on that subject in the Newark Public Library where I spent my youthful Exile. So now David Gascoyne's reference is noted between the parenthesis of "birth" and "death" dates.

I am drowsy, falling almost to sleep now—it is about 10 p.m.—under the spell of a young woman violinist playing Sarasate's *Malaqueña* on the classical music station (Capitol Public Radio-FM) here in Stocktonia. Why do people live in Kentucky? I have always thought of that State, the "blue-grass State" as inhabited possibly by Centaurs, race horses, and *blue* as opposed to green grass I'd have preferred Al-Ghazzali to be African descended in the line of my Ethiopic forebears, of the Queen of Sheba, but alas he wasn't be that as it may "A man must indeed become truly poor and as free from his own creaturely will as he was when he was born," so says the great Eckhart Mystic and I am sure the Mystic in the soul of David Grascoyne resounds to these words as do I . . .

It was Meister Eckhart who said that not Al-Ghazzali. *Midi au Dimanche* (Sunday afternoon) again failed to journey out of doors because of agoraphobic fit (And if there's a Reader out there let him or her know I am also unable to drive to for both nervous-disorder as well as economic reasons) Had it in mind to take my church *Leaves of Grass* along with me as a companion on that walk but that, too, annulled.

READING FROM THE ANGEL HAIR ANTHOLOGY, AD 2001, SAN FRANCISCO

Quatrains for Anne's Birthday

for Anne Waldman

"l' union par l 'Amour l' Union Amour"
  —L. S. Senghor

A man's lost his head and run away
In your direction again
Like St. Dionysios (*Saint Dénis*)
A piece

Of evidence in the shape (*Africa remembers*)
of a torn envelope   Just talked to Bob
        (Rauschenberg's) surrogate Ramona on the phone
this morning to tell her

I'll send you the reflection in the mirror
of that lovely leggy French lass
on the TV *ROC* commercial   (you see,
there are "uses" for even TV commercials—Although

Befittingly she should be the inhabitant
of a *schloss*   of Rilke's in the *Duino*
And here to be noted, "uses" is such a crass
allusion anyway   It happens at moments like this

I pause pensively like Diego
Rivera must have done in the midst of working on his Rockefeller
Center Murals in elephantine overalls
with that *Non Serviam* look

As he stares into the future   Of which
I will remain as who I am now and as
I "was" And where the name
of Anne will be forever

Introduction to (MY) Théâtres
(AD 1966–2007)

On the *Theatre of the Absurd*, "In Media Res"

As for the term itself it was coined by—to my knowledge—critic Martin Esslin in his book of the same title (1961). But for me, *Theatre of the Absurd*—as well as Le Surrealisme Meme—always begins with Apollinaire in his *Breasts of Tiresias*, performed in Paris, June 24, 1917: his poem–play announced for the first time un drame surréaliste. All hell breaks loose thereafter.

What I want to say is: "It" begins here. But then the usual difficulty arises: there is always another antecedent, in effect, one finds one is always in the midst with no beginning; and what it "means" to "begin" eventually alludes all the "way back" to the "Big Bang" itself! All the speculations then devolve, if you will, around cosmology: Bambara, Platono–Aristotelian Or that of *Lemaitre's*.

The "Unhappy Consciousness" as Hegel articulated in his ground-breaking *Phenomenology*, aspires to be independent of the material world (and might we say also the "Material Girl" *Madonna*?) to go forth unto the resemblance of the Creator, in other words, to be "eternal and purely spiritual; yet at the same time recognizing its physical desires, pains, pleasures, are, in the end, "real and inescapable." As a result the Unhappy Consciousness is divided against itself. It appears this last statement is the crux of the matter. Here we have the beginning of the modern disconcertion of "being-in-the-world," Self (Hegel's *selbst*), and Other, the game Sartre is already playing with his characters before we know it, a kind of tiddlywinks, but with little actual play, *ludens*, fun, reflecting the author–philosoph's stern Calvinist background,—no humor, no fun, no clowning around no *slapstick* (à la Charlie Chaplin) such as we might see in *Godot*/Beckett.

Confessio Amantis: When I was a boy, mere stripling, I revelled in the antics of "Mr. Television," Milton Berle on TV (I think it was each Tuesday night?) vying inexorably with the Grey Eminence pronouncements of Bishop Fulton J. Sheen. (I could compensate, however, finding Sheen's books in the library and being awed by his knowledge of philosophy and literature) (I envied his *Agrégé*, Doctor of Philosophy, from Louvain!) But it was "Uncle Milty" who embodied me for Poetry.

Yet I was amazed at Bishop Sheen's vignettes from Dostoyevsky (*The Brothers Karamazov*) and his thorough knowledge of Thomas Aquinas's *Summa* (which I also happened to be studying at the time about age 18 or so).

Sheen's weekly talks on TV led me to explore the waywardness of the modern temper, its *Angst*—Auden's *Age of Anxiety* and Eliot's *Cocktail Party*—the sense of separation from the flow of the cosmos which so characterised the "on the go" temperament of American society where I found myself with Thoreau listening to the "sound of a distant drummer." Yet in the end preferred the mad antics of Milton Berle ("Uncle Milty") to the wise pronouncements of the *Grey Eminence* (Bishop Sheen). And the Unhappy Consciousness found itself dancing to a slapstick tune with me.

I was in SU REAL ITY before I knew but only found out its "official" capacity with Breton much later. For the time being travelled *Terra Incognita*—Until I realized I was in the *royaume* de Poésie (domain of poetry)

With all my faux pas and blunders warmly welcomed by (French) Surrealism.

I then found Poetry and Theatre to be virtually one and the same, the latter requiring (at times) an Actor and/or Actress or other characters, two or three perhaps, talking trees, smug Generals strolling across the stage with unravelling rolls of toilet paper; some women's high-heeled shoes left on stage (without feet in them) allowed to speak for themselves—with the aid and encouragement of the Poet!

But Big Bang was always looming there in the background with Uncle Milty Berle and even with His Grey Eminence, Bishop Sheen.

—On TV the new theatre of the Absurd is the show *The View* courtesy Barbara Walter's & Co.—

Consider: The *Comoedia Del'Arte* thriving during the fires of the Inquisition and our era of VCR's, decibels, sex shops, and Racial Profiling in America of the Twenty-First Century in the wake of the insanity of "9/11" and its toxic mythos created by the Power Elite to justify its reign and silencing of all Dissent in America where Yours Truly happens to find himself. So the Unhappy Consciousness continues to distend and *T-W-A-N-G!*

The Word "Pansophic," as Voiced by Sally Forth in the Sunday Comics

Pansophy, "universal wisdom—pansophic"—*Random House Dictionary of the American Language*

On the word, "Pansophic," then. As we spoke the other day, "Writing as we know it today was the outgrowth of the invention of *cuneiform* by ancestors in Iraq (the former Babylon-Assyria)/ It is all to their credit that I struggled for two hours with contorted typewriter ribbon and blackened fingertips today—and yes, it is *supposed* to be "a day of rest" according to the Judeo-Christian Bible and we won't go "into" what the Buddhists believe, since they don't celebrate a Sabbath, nor what the adherents of Islam hold to ("business as usual" on a Sunday in Cairo, for instance) but you know it hasn't changed there's no vacation or holiday for the poet from poetry really as the ovum continues to be manufactured in the reproductive organs of the female and sperm in the organ of the male I haven't interviewed a single sperm or ovum who hasn't testified this to be so   On the other hand contrary to public opinion I haven't interviewed any "little green men" lately either, although according to Roswell (New Mexico) they wouldn't know very much as they aren't green and have no genitalia to speak of

At this moment in the mind of every bird is the thought of the long journey "flying South" must preoccupy but at the same time doesn't preoccupy *my* thoughts as I can't fly and I am about as far "South" as I care to be at this time thank you without heading into the endless Los Angeles Freeway the thought of which stirs up my agoraphobic angst But it doesn't end there no not "by a long shot" you'll find the whole of human history in the stacks of papers and books piled on my bed from which I've just fallen off in the dark interim (*KABOOM!*)

Malmaisonique

for Mlle. Kristin Prevallet

qui cherche son chemin . . . dans quelque clairiere perdue de moi
—Léopold Sédar Senghor

I say there where you are   *rassemblement*

roses of the Empress Josephine trail your robe

                    As I like Eurydice's representative
turn
round   my hands as emissaries to your realm
                as that princess of Egypt found
the infant Moses's boat of bullrushes

"in the blink of an eye"
a lighthouse in my room (rather diffident)
A woman's chosen in the TV studio audience
          with the "winning number 89"

Felix Rohatyn "Friend of France"

Each attempt of my letter turns into an antiphon

Handel's *Music for the Royal Fireworks*
          cours of Sergi's *in altre* regioni dell
                              l'Abissini

Your slipper with its flamingo flourish
passes by in midair   with so many stories to tell

NOTE: *Malmaisonique: Malmaison*, palace near Paris where the Empress
Josephine lived after her divorce from the Emperor Napoleon. There is a
beautiful park connected with Malmaison containing beautiful trees and
varieties of roses that Josephine planted there.

130

Just Come from Delivering a Lecture on the Origins of Russian Literature . . .

And a banana was right in the middle of the parking lot and I had to kick it away in the process I hear Britney (Spears) has had yet another breakdown in public and shed her clothes and she never received my letter on the benefits of listening to the *Overture to Prince Igor* by Borodin and I've just told the clerk at the grocery store who complained about "the nasty customers" this morning, "Keep a water pistol (loaded) behind your counter and spray them to cool them off" Then thought of that banana peel left lying there in the middle of the street in the parking lot perhaps I hadn't kicked it off that well in the first place it might be still lying where it shouldn't where an unsuspecting pedestrian could take a nose dive off it but then it's too late it's already a mile and half behind me on the walk home (here, too, is your perennial pedestrian) oops did I say the word "home" which isn't really mine after all but use it here as an "euphemism," as a place to "hang my hat" (and coat as well, although we surely don't need coats in this weather!) I talk to the mailbox but know it won't answer me Another thought about "Achilles' heel" Am wondering how Thetis (his mom) must have held him as an infant dunking him in the river to keep him "invulnerable" to mortal blows Now someone's holding an ice pack to his head (scenario on one of the Soap Operas on TV don't recall which) One thing we know "for certain" it's not Hallowe'en as yet nor is this a "Palimpsest" Well here's a letter in the post from a man who says he'll make me "rich in only a few short months" by following his "method" It *isn't* the *Stanislavsky Method*, that's for sure If these letters were sent out all over the country then by now we'd have "a booming economy" but I'm afraid the evidence is against it by now my "train of thought" is somewhere in Kansas just as *Dorothy's house* flies by (12:54 p.m.) After taking inventory I have returned with all the clothes on my back that I started out with

Dream. (December 20, AD 2002): I Received a Cake of Ice Formed of the Early Auden's words . . ..

I received a cake of ice formed of the early Auden's words, "We must love another or die." It was in the shape of a largish English dictionary which could fit into a pouch. How this came to be I don't know but it was meant to be a talisman for the age where I lived and I was to be its conservateur. The block of ice, however, had the same qualities of any other frozen liquid:—it could melt, even as I held it it already began to dissolve in drops; drops of the precious frozen verbiage were now in a trail of water wherever I went; I was on foot, I could not drive and made plans to head for home as soon as possible before the gift I held dissolved into nothing. It so happened I was in England, at Cambridge, I believe, which was where I came into possession of the block of ice.

So I quickly consulted a group of Mathematics professors who were strolling by as to what I should do in this situation where I found myself (I assumed they were Mathematics professors they had that kind of aura) One of them wryly told me, "Look here, old chap, whichever way you turn, your ice, no matter how honoured or magical, will surely melt in the end and you'll be left with nothing unless you get to a freezer right away". With that swish of self-importance the gentlemen professor turned to his colleagues garbed in their traditional gowns and they were off into the distance. Just then I noticed some Students passing by, stopping one of them, a pretty young woman, asking her if she might give me a lift so that I could deposit the ice in my freezer, remonstrating to her that my block of ice was quickly melting. She seemed to snicker, "*What on earth* are you doing, Sir, walking about with a block of ice!?" I could see then that even she was about to dismiss me thinking this was some sort of practical joke. I tried to engage her in conversation as long as I could, hoping—against hope—as it were—that somehow I might convince her that my story was indeed true and perhaps secure a ride home to store my block of ice, which I noticed by now was diminishing to the size of an ordinary book, seeping through the paper bag container.

"Well, this may be hard to believe," I began, as my Student furrowed her brow and had a smirk on her lips, "Oh, yes?" I explained, "But you see this block of ice is special, it's formed of the early Auden's words, "We must love one another or die."

"You have got to be joking or have been missing appointments with your psychiatrist. Now do please excuse me as I must be going to class—I'm late now as it is—Sorry." "Ah, don't go just yet, I swear what I've been telling you *is* true. I don't know how it happened but I've been entrusted with this thing and . . . I'm supposed to be its conservateur for the ages." She swerved, stopping her bike, looking back at me, "Well, even if I did believe you and your story, as you see I have no car here and I don't want to take a chance on my bike holding two riders—it's not safe, really. Sorry, you'll have to look for someone else to help you, I'm afraid," as she brushed back wisps of her long brown hair that had blown in her face, stepped on the pedals and was off in a flash. Left there standing, I could feel the weight of my precious parcel grow less and less. I was afraid to open the bag and look into it. I was somehow fortunate, though, as on this occasion it became suddenly overcast—I looked up wondering if this were some kind of "sign" . . .. As I stood there right in the midst of the Student commons, students in their black gowns whooshed about everywhere on their bikes about me, as I tried to signal one of them to stop, but thought I'd be met with the same attitude of incredulity and would be back where I started from in this dilemma.

If I walked forward the ice would continue to dissolve. If I remained where I stood I would find my ice-block of the early Auden's words but a puddle of water, and I thus would fail as the appointed conservateur of the ages.

At that point it seemed everything came to a standstill. The students appeared like statues immobilized on their bikes. A don's robe frozen in its flutter in the wind. I was the only one moving with the bag of ice continuing to drips its precious contents, the liquefied words of the Poet, "We must love one another or die." I gathered enough courage to look into the bag at the block of ice; the words were still *there!*—but for how long? Given the status of affairs about me, human assistance was now out of the question. A dog, a stray, or so I surmised, happened to come along—the only being mobile except myself (How was it everything was frozen in time but this one creature?) The dog began licking up the trail of liquid seeping from my bag. The dog looked up at me and smiled. "I *have* your solution," the dog said. (I thought to myself, how could this be, but then, everything else was completely out of the ordinary, so I listened.) "I've been walking for more than an hour looking for something to drink and now you have provided it for me," replied the dog, looking up at me, waiting for my response.

"Well, I don't know what to say . . ."

Ah, ah, but you don't understand, I—I—was made conservateur of this block of ice which isn't at all ordinary, it's very special, formed of a poet's words, you see, it's meant to be a sign for the ages . . ."

"Ah, but I *do* understand," said the dog, his gaze intensified as he spoke,—he seemed a common "mutt" variety—but cute. I surveyed the scene about me: cyclist, students and profs still frozen as statues caught on their way to this or that appointment, I wondered how long it had been that I had stood there—an hour—or two—*ten, fifteen minutes?*—my own sense of time was dissolved.

The dog, continuing to look up at me, "Look, you *have* accomplished what you have set out to do . . ."

"What do you mean, I don't see that. Would you mind explaining, please?"

"You *are* the conservateur of these words and *I am the ages.*"

"*Wha* . . . Excuse me, you said . . . ?"

"You've heard correctly, *er*, right from the dog's mouth!"

At that moment I felt the package I was carrying become suddenly weightless. Feeling dejected in spite of the encouragement offered by the dog, I thought, "Oh no, this is *it*, I've failed in my mission. Had I only hurried along right from the beginning . . . I would most likely have succeeded in preserving this block of ice with its words for the ages . . . I looked down at my feet the dog was now slurping up the last drops of the liquid that had once been my prized block of ice. the dog looked up at me then and said, "Look, don't worry, it's okay. All has been accomplished here. Thank You." I was puzzled at this but then the revelation came to me, as the dog said, "Your words have been *delivered to me*: your words have been delivered to *the ages which is myself,* 'We must love one another or die.'"

Une Jeune Femme Africaine

... *Qui cherche son chemin et se lamente dans quelque clairière perdu
de moi—L. S. Senghor, Poèmes Divers*

And this morning I thought the sea was in my room
Or was it I in a room of the sea   And the star which you wore
in that spurious moment hung there   above the ruminations
of the sea which were plush   For this anchorite, then
it came to me once again the vision of the *Sable Venus* arriving
barefoot with her retinue across the billows sound of
Applause from a concert of Mozart sonatas (across the
                              piano keys the fingers of Alicia
                                      de Larrocha   dance)
By now would say "Arabia Felix" as opposed to Infelix
For once Arabia was "happy" at the silver filigree broadcast from
your dress your bois *d' ébène* and sandalwood nakedness
I meet my audience   Time   Language   History   which
give their testimony through you
Not one of your svelte limbs knows the word "cruel"

And the hour "that in which   the heart is always   full"

NOTE: *Qui cherche son chemin* . . . that which searches its way in a clearing
lost with a lament within myself

Poem Begun at the End

Begin,then !
My hand   send out   your vesper sentinel
            to explore   the fine terrrain of

Her nightgown   roseate vapoure of Chinese silk

        —Yet consider cuneiform crushed under
tank treads in Iraq—What
Assyrian poet will write on *that* ?

Can the whole world
be summed up in six lines—or less?
(Galileo's telescope width
        of no more than five inches   gave us gallaxies
But the name of his only daughter shrouded
    in nunnery's obscurity)

Here and now I write   the Poem's beginning
from its ending   My hand evokes
Song as it runs along my Cushitic beard

. . . that cause and effect must be . . .

        As I pull open the drawstring
to the morning's scape
The blinds scream
        In the bowl of oatmeal is *Mayakovsky's brain !

NOTE: *Mayakovsky, Vladimir Mayakovski *1893–1930*, Russian avant-garde
poet and Bolshevik. Visited Paris and met with French Surrealist Poets
there, 1924.

The Dogs of Baghdad Are Barking

for Ms. Lara Logan, BBC

The dogs of Baghdad are barking startled
by successive explosions in the City
A young girl is just waking in her pajamas
The President has announced he
and the First Lady will retire for the evening   It is early
still in the morning *there* A reporter on TV news has the hiccups

I would have hiccups too if I were *there*

I have just dined on salad on the rim of the bowl
a fly has alighted and takes off again I hear
the echo

of my neighbor's high-heeled shoes on her hardwood
floor upstairs But the only echo I continue to hear is that of
the dogs of Baghdad barking on TV this evening
startled by the noise the rose and the flame-imploding skies of the City
Subtitles on the screen announce "Programming
changes" I am now in my pajamas Attention Cashiers

in the interminable yoked
sky and ravine

The dogs of Baghdad are barking

A Man Is Riding the Head of
Saddam Hussein in Baghdad

for Lara Logan

A man is riding the head of Saddam Hussein in Baghdad
Right now   how many are thinking
about their *diet?*   (possibly few if any)
And it is true, nowhere in the sky
or in the trees will you find a master clock that predicts
the measure of time for us

       As *"Uncle Ez'" recounts, "Basil kept
the name of *Firdousi
       nailed to his door"   name of the central
Square in Baghdad   The "Elvis factor"
Spotted here spotted there   I made a fire
the azure having left me
in my living room . . . Only weeks before on TV
an *M-1* tank rolled and parked
in moonlight beside a ziggurat.

NOTES:

Uncle Ez', American poet, Ezra Pound (*1885–1972*) as he liked to be
familiarly referred to by his circle of friends. The reference is taken from his
Pisan Cantos, Canto *LXXVII*, "Firdush on His door"

فردوش Persian poet, author of the *ShahNameh*, Firdousi, Abou I₁ Qasim
IlMansour, AD 940–1020, wrote the national epic of Iran, in *FARSI*; works
translated into Arabic.

On Pierre's Birthday, 19 September AD 2003

à Mme. Sandra Morînaud

De sa grâce redoutable
—Paul Valéry, *Charmes*

African gladiolas make their way up just now in the garden

        From underground as they hear
a *chacun*   from Jean Philippe Rameau coming from the window
open here in California
Hooray The Communist Party is 84 years young

                One of Fourier's *Transforms*
a "sinusoid" refugee as it so happens in my room speaks only
Chinese

(As can be inferred our conversation doesn't go very far)

Highlight of the day   *Mrs.* Monet emerging   as Aurora
glides over the meadow with her parasol

The TV Weathergirl   attired in bright red chemise
In Rome my brother Tarun sleeps snoring away (much to the
annoyance of his wife, Paola)
The little girl who once purred in the courtyard in Mountain View
      "¿Tiene gatitos?"   is now about 23—somewhere

The poet who defends the power structure
becomes a turnip
      Du Bonheur La Vie Cinématique
Exiled   forever from   *Serendip*

لسَرً نلپِ

[(Farsi)-Ser-endip]

139

Manifeste

Who Speaks ? Out of airy nothing in
The empty Boardroom   The Voice
Of Bartolomeo Vanzetti I address you Gentlemen and Gentlewomen
And the rough seas of the Channel Crossing
(June 6th, 1944)   And here the ground
Where Crazy Horse met his end   It was

Only yesterday when I thought
I had nothing "left" to say

And I let myself be taken over by the green

Of the tree outside my window

        Where it seemed I had watched for hours   consoling
myself with writing letters
To Dante   And you hills who should be up now
and skipping like rams
It's a workday

We can look back fondly on an era
        when stealing hubcaps off of cars was the rage   Establish
tents of victory through the samoyed's blue eyes
As yet my guitar string
severed across the *GNP graph-line

NOTE: *GNP (Gross National Product)

Rendez-vous du Dimanche (10 heures au matin)

for Kaithlin

Voici la poésie se matin . . .
—Apollinaire, *Zone*

"Doors of the future" open for the June Graduate

But not for the Poet
As you juggle "a barista" now running the café's errands
                    for "supplies" in this moment as I behold

Colchis in your flaxen hair

The imagination introduces itself an alien
To your domain this Sunday a long way from Montparnasse poetry
takes momentary residence in your name

And again I am confronted with
the same
            You don't know   who
Arshille Gorky is

                        And the whole task thereafter
seems almost like a rehabilitation
Or at best a resettlement (more or less)
of all that which must
                        "people" your mind
I have a diagram here of some basic   yogic morning

Exercises that I never use
Soon the Sahara will be paying
its daily visit to my room   As I tell you *Doonesbury*

                                    Has all   the answers
But first I
must find the questions   Then there
you are
a little, far-off   star in "A galaxy far away"

But actually in the next township of Tokay

Poetry Is This Hall of Mirrors "est de celles qui n'ont pas fait leur chemin"

—Manifeste Politique de Surrealistes, Paris, 1931

Poetry is this My coming to you knowing who I am not knowing who I am Is you coming to me knowing who you are not knowing who you are in this Hall of Mirrors Poetry is this coming together knowing who we were Not knowing who we are Poetry Is this We who are coming together knowing who we are not knowing who we are We who are coming together knowing who we are not knowing who we are who come together knowing who we are not knowing who we are And yes outside the window a church is galloping While we are coming together knowing knowing who we are not knowing who we are knowing who we are in this Hall of Mirrors I do not know why This Is

For Sandy Berrigan: "(Another) Possible Story of My Life"

(*Another*)   (Possible)   "Story of My Life" arises, it seems
    each time
I reach for   a piece of paper (it   (vanishes)
        a few side dishes, such as
                    Garlic Mashed Potatoes
                       Envoy
"*C*" from the Cookie Monster
Now we   *segué*   to *La Jugement De Paris*

Who sits there quite undisturbed quite naked
            before the Three Goddesses
as he holds the golden apple
        Absent   from the scene are
            Andy Rooney   Vladimir
Mayakovsky
and Africa   I don't know where to go "next"

—With *Fourier Transforms*, that is to say   Are the *sinusoids*
"real" ?) Empty vistas grey skies rooms stairways
    ἡ ὕλη (Matter)   μορφή (Form) ἡ ἰδέα (Appearances)

On the TODAY SHOW a woman outside holds a sign at the
window that says "Be A DO-er!" If Ted were here I'd
hand it to him as the first line
        for his latest poem

For Dave Humphreys (AD 1951–2008), Poet, Stockton, California

"Love should walk throughout the entire Universe!"
 —Vladimir Mayakovsky

Before I go out
to the post box   to find yet another letter
returned to me
from CHINA (written in Chinese—how did
it get past the Post Office to be "delivered"
Here in Stockton, Calif.?)
         My authority for
Mandarin remains the lovely
Ms. Anna Naruta of
         Oakland
(I don't know about her proficiency in Cantonese, however)
Mia Farrow and Maria Contrarez-Something-or-Other are
appearing in Sacramento for Woman's Day Something
to my knowledge none of these
         know Chinese

However I *can* guarantee you
my name is *not* *Ned Ludd

I am actually (to counter Milton) of Mayakovsky's
and *Krazy Kat's* Party "**è quei che più allegrezza sente*"

         *"who sends forth his utmost cheer"
         (—Guido Cavalcanti)

NOTE: *Ned Ludd*, fictitious name given by Luddites opposing
technological innovation of the Industrial Revolution in England, circa
1811–1812.

POETRY=THE SNUFFALAPAGUS

What's Happening inside Her Haute-Couture Shoes

for Joyce Kulhawik

Angels winging their way   Westward the vermillion
Imprint of Nico's kiss of the Velvet Underground
De Sade's whips converted into Lilies of the Nile
swaying caresses   The map of France intones
its secret grottoes   rainbow colours   Lucy-Sur-Yonne   Cluny

There the nose of Cyrano my patron saint
                ever on the path of pilgrimage   *In her path*

now down the aisles of the supermart   packages of cereal

                                        fly off the shelves
at her arrival to become her Honour Guard with crossed swords

To the theme music written in the Forbidden City of the Chinese
                                Emperor Han Chou

For there I can say the "Velvet Revolution" (of Vacláv Havel)
begins here as the sequestered
                beauty of woman's toes

substitutes henceforth as the exchange for money bread for the hungry

And here all the greatness of ideas
        of the "heavenly city" of the philosophers Africa sends
its prince's mantle of "wax and gold" *Delle Meravigilla*
Once more in the tenderness of the doe that comes out of hiding
to drink at the sacred spring

Poem for Isabel Allende That Still Remains Unfinished

How many times   was it started and had to be abandoned
packed up in a suitcase, which wasn't always
a suitcase but more likely
a cardboard box or large plastic leaf bag
being rushed from place to place   I have more
than one "invented country"
if you must know   my only "real" country is

In the Arabic script of Ibn Al Arbi and then
in the shimmer of a passing girl's hair

Perhaps my "true" country is the morning *Amanecer*
(Although, even of that I can never be sure)

The *accent grave*   or *aigu*   Or *point virgule*
the name Sinclaire Beiles named his shortlived review
my poems however never found their way there)
                    Or the barely audible
          breaths of Glenn Gould inhaled and exhaled between
notes performing his Bach *French Suite No. 5*

                              Yet a part of me will
always remain in the bunker of *La Moneda* in the dark
approach of Fall (1973) As well clothes in sun facing the picture-
wall-length window in the parlour of the Joseph Hoffman House
in October as the vermillion sea of leaves rushed in

NOTE: *La Moneda*, Santiago, Chile, where the president, Salvador Allende
fell defending democracy against the fascist forces of General Pinochet
aided by U.S. CIA. 1973 President Allende was uncle of author Isabel
Allende. The *Joseph Hoffman House*, located in New City, New York State,
built in 1920s; classic modern architectural "icon"; S. T. guest there of Lita
and Morton Hornick in 1976. One of the homes in United States of the
Hornick family, the home has been featured throughout the years in
Architectural Digest.

(FURTHER) NOTE: (AHK sohn)

Accent grave (grAH-V) accent aigu; point virgule

French accents: *grave; aigu* (Ah-gheW); *point virgule* (PWAhn Veergyule); *grave; aigu;* over vowels indicates closed or open sounds in French; *point (et) virgule* (PWahn-t virgyule) indicates semicolon; punctuation

For My Friend, the Incomparable
Nanos Valaoritis, Poet

*and for my friends of the Greek Surrealist Group, Dino Siotis, Gianni
Chioles, Odysseos Élytis, Nikos Engonópoúlos*

Grèce ma rose de raison
—Paul Éluard

In te mi getto . . . di navate posa nel cuore
—Salvatore Quasimodo, *Alla Mia Terra*

I hear the Greek National Hymn
of Solomos play on
in my head
And the word
Missoluonghi
repeats continually inside
myself no matter where I may go
And there   eyes of the child *Fotini Léonidópolóu*
before me   her gaze is ever into
the future I say that one day she will create

(A thousand years from Today

I see the monument erected to her
in the *Plaka*)
And an invisible rose
goes out once again
          to place

In Hommage

at the stele   dedicated to Lord Byron

Whose remains lie in the land he loved

And *Kekrops
also who before the written word
arrived from *l'Afrique* to lay the foundations
in Hellas
That torch   which now cicumnavigates
the world
            from Olympia (There
      where beautiful maidens stand today with naked feet
the hem of their gowns' flutter

Across my
blank page   in the stillness of the morning

"A hard task master"

The Poem
that waits in ambush before I leave the door

NOTES:

For Incomparable Nanos . . .

Mentre l' Italia e la Grecia e poi l'Africa
settentrionale contengono la massima parte
dei loro primitivi abitatori . . .. le recchie tombe
che hanno sato luce gli avanzi umani

—Guiseppi Sergi, *Africa Antropologie*
Roma, 1897

Kekrops (*Κέκρωψ*)
Mythic Founder of Athens. *Kekrops*, represented as
having the form of a man with that of a serpent,
emigrated from Africa to become the first king of Attica.
The *Kekropia*, upon which the Acropolis is laid, is named
after him. *Kekrops introduced the art of writing to
the Greeks* as well as agriculture and the institution
of marriage.

Salvatore Quasimodo (1901–1968)
Italian poet. Of *Sicilian origin, Greek and Moorish-Arab descent* from the Island, Quasimodo taught Greek and
Classics. An opponent of the Fascist regime, the poet
joined the Communist Party and the Resistance during World War II.
La Terra Impreggiable (1955) contains a number of poems
devoted to Greece. He received the Nobel Prize for Literature
in 1959.

Greek Surrealist Group. While André Breton negated the poetic influence
of the Classical Civilisations of the Mediterranean, embracing
rather old Gallic and other exotic sources in the quest of the Marvelous,
Greek poets in the 1930s formed their own version of
the Surrealist Group. These originally included George Seferis
as well as Odysseos Elytis, amongst others. Greek Surrealists
embraced the efficacy of their own Mediterranean culture and
mythos, thus differing from their French counterparts. During
the 1960s the works of Odysseos Elytis and Nanos Valaoritis
emerged and these poets became as mentors to the younger generation
of Greek writers. Members of the younger generation of
Greek Surrealist poets, Gianni Chioles and Dino Siotis, became
exiles, protesting the Fascist Junta of the 1970s,
forming a group about the poet Nanos Valaoritis in San Francisco.

<u>ENIGMA OF PRINCE MYSHKIN</u> . For Antoinette .

I don 't know why

but it seems   I 'm more tired
each time I get out of bed nowadays. I feel more religion
in music than in my bones
or in any church. I know ....
I' m reduced to this nothing I ' ve
finally come about to discern
            Of that generation that remembers
Paul Winchell and ventriloquist's dummy , Jerry Mahoney
              (a replica doll of which I once
          owned in childhood)   soup priced
at .35 !   one could then simply take down a can
from the stockpile of canned goods in the larder
At the same time thinking
of your face, its beauty being

The transit between Earth and Heaven ... still inside the
desk drawer is the Blackamoor
who would give you crocheting lessons

                    S. T.
                    April ,AD2004

153

A Man's Voice Answers on Her Cell Phone

And it is undoubtedly *not* the Gobi Desert
(*Ah, that it were!*) not the horse voice of the Dalai Lama . . .
It is undoubtedly that of her lover
    A police-car siren punctuates the heavy air of the summer night
In one year perhaps I will have forgotten this night (At least
this is what I tell myself I will have relegated it to nothing-
ness)
    But now I realize I have in my adumbrations missed the *Nightly
Business Report* on TV, nonetheless we can assume that the "world situation"
remains as is as unstable as ever (ah yes, whensoever *was*
the world "stable" ?)
    My Thanks to you O Olympean Mallarmé, you who knew the height
was inaccessible yet dared the ascent only to acknowledge failure
each time, I clutch your book to myself—In lieu of holding
her, that is
    Alba the dawn which lovers dread but I shall not have to worry
about *that*
    I am now actually "feeling" the distance grow between us (It
began the moment of my call when the stranger's voice answered in
lieu of hers) as when standing on the beach the pull of the tide away
the whole of the world being pulled away   Were I still on the "Great
White Way" of Broadway I would have felt just as displaced or even
so at the *Gard du Nord*
    The "man on the street"   has never heard of the "Elephants'
Burial Ground" (Its site still remains undisclosed in Africa)
but that stranger's voice emanating from her boudoir would surely
desecrate that pachyderm's repose

Another "certainty"—had she and I allowed into each other's
history—she certainly would have defeated me at chess!
That silence our hands still clasp in a nomadic ionic exchange
(her own pursuit of "economics and world religions", her espousal
of the rights of "prisoners of conscience") All of which illumined
by Eros

    The two precipices in this gulf (*gouffre*) : vanity with its
ridiculous headdress and ambition with its laughter about the barbecue
on the patio while Orion continues to chase the Pleiades
across the night sky

On the Wall in My Room . . .
The Photo of Lenin

On the wall in my room Lenin addresses History and thousands of years of oppression   The photo is still yet I can see him move and gesture to the crows below, swaggering and swaying as he speaks   as in a holograph   I can hear his words surmount the world's Babel, Uighur,   Uzbek, Cicero's Latin, Old High Slavonic, Arabic   French   Armenian (Eastern and Western branches)   Castillian, even German (which was Marx's language throughout his life as well as his compère, Engels). Mallarme would have some difficulty with this as the poet championed the hermetic and certainly not the crowd but would this not equally have applied to the "mad" Dane, Hamlet, and is he not too an allegory for the state of humanhood on the Planet in search of itself   to be *reconstituted*?

And there in Vienna (*Wien*) *Freud's couch* sprouts its wings like a fledgling bird first learning how to spring from the comfort of its nest. . . .

In Tel Aviv a young woman's lithe body shimmers bronzed from the sun as she showers   her long hair the colour of honey glides over her bare shoulders Only missing is someone   to sing her the *Song of Songs* (her body more sacred than any temple or synagogue those who would venture upon her should know. Hers are thousands and thousands of prototypes

As I say 'Thank You for your service,' to my pen as it is empty of its ink.

Yet from the photo of Lenin on my wall speaking to the crowds in Petrograd Lenin's words go round the globe like Columbus's caravels in search for the New World

And yes the Ocean still seems endless O on then to the Continent where "C I V I L A S A T I O N" began Where W. E. B. DuBois's remains are now interred Where Nelson Mandela kept a small garden during his years of imprisonment
(And the words came there and embedded themselves)
Africa   shall yet ascend
Lenin's words   stand by the twelve-year-old Palestinian who watches as his family's ancestral home is demolished in a moment in East Jerusalem (within sight of the Wailing Wall) as the Occupiers of the land declare the home "a refuge for terrorists" I hear alone in my room Lenin's words resound above the demolition of the site

(As the Muezzin calls the Faithful to prayer and bells of the Catholic church sound

Ur That Is No Longer There

for Philip Lamatia

"Un Araméen errant était mon père"
—*Deuteronome 26:5*

Though the Leonid Meteor Shower still passes overhead
there   It is no longer *Ur*
Though the land abide
furrows of tank-tracks and assault
It is no longer *Ur*.
Once, Friend, You thought of journeying there
To *Ur* that is no longer *Ur*.
Had I been able to I would have made that journey
with you there

But that dream is now faded into actors' thin air

We are such
stuff as
that Ur is no longer "there"

If I but sit here cloistered in the same
scribbles and scrawls that covered
                            pages of Beethoven's manuscript
notes of music
I am closer to the *Ur* that
                     was once there

I speak for the oriflamme *faire-la-cour*
honour
of France and the kingdom
of the seahorse Thus
in kissing the hand of the beautiful woman
this Sunday I am to the *Ur*
that is no longer there

an Emissary who impugns
war its designers and think-tank devisers and enactors

O winged bulls that once surveilled

The westward trek of Aram
beneath a crescent moon in the company of Blackamoor brothers
and sisters
From the gates of *Ur*
an *Ur* that is no longer *there*
—*Levez-vous*
et Allons!
Arise
Let us be on our way

FROM MY JOURNAL : 3 February AD2005

" What a Poet 's Life Is " Like" "

    I had to go out at 5 A.M. this morning to purchase toilet paper
(we had completely run out ; my daughtervhad forgotten to tell me
and I myself hadn 't bothered to look into the supply bin in the bath-
room.) So , flashlight (torch) in hand I found myself out on the road.
The fog was so thick here in the Valley Of The San Joaquin I could hardly
see beyond my nose! (Yours Truly is a pedestrian without a car and also
being an agoraphobe who has to down two shots of brandy before emerging out-
of-doors to dispel the symptoms of my disorder, the whole question of
driving remains non-applicable in my case.)
    I have made it to the local Shopping Centre nearby and the Safeway
open 24-hours here. Seeing that there didn 't seem to be any check-out
clerks at the front registers, I asked a packer stacking items on the shelves
store shelves-- remember this is 5 A.M. !--about the availability of
a cashier to service me. The young fellow was rather burly and brusque
head-shaven tatooed working on the aisle and he gave out at that moment
a rather bad-tempered shout to the checker approaching (I was as far as I
could see the only customer extant in the store at the time) and the
young woman emerged from the far end doors of the stock -room rushing
up to the check-out stand. As I moved my grocery cart forward with its
econ Econ-pack of toilet paper toward her station, I could see she was
disgruntled at being yelled at by her co-worker. I smiled as she
"scanned" my items for the pricing-- I had accumulated a few other things
while waiting in the aisle -- and she smiled back , more at ease now:
"I 'm sorry you had to be yelled at by that guy but I couldn 't see
anyone up at the check-out counter to help me. "
" Oh, that 's okay , I don 't mind , we yell at each other all the time",
she said as she bagged my items and handed over the large package of
toilet paper to me as I got out my ATM card to pay for my things.
The young woman was an Afro-American person with skin complexion not much
different than my own. The co-worker who summoned her so brusquely was
a white male whom I might have inferred as a " biker-type". My checker
smiled once again as she totalled the sale and I Thanked her cordially
wishing her a good day (hoping she wouldn 't have to be summoned again
by her less-than-gracious co-worker) as I left the store and out again
in the midst of the fog, I still felt a bit groggy from lack of sleep
and thought to myself," All of this seems so futile, but perhaps I was
meant to be there just to give the check-out girl a smile and some
fellow-feeling in showing my appreciation and wishing her well."
    Toilet paper under my arm and plastic bag I tread on"home."
                    -- Sotère Torregian
                       3e febrier AD2005
                       Stockton , Calif.

158

For Pierre and Sandra Morinaud

Le Bonheur Happiness Is

Le Bonheur   Happiness is

knocking at your door   even   now (it doesn't stop)

As I sit here typing on   Anya's high-school typewriter
(vintage 1956 ?)   *Halloo !*

Playing hide-and-seek through
the shower door
My block of cuneiform seems to have vanished
again   from where it once sat   proudly   at the top
of my desk. I don't suppose
it has wanted to migrate back to *Baghdad ?*

While the second knock at the door   is a bone

    From Tombouctou   clothed for its appearance
in a robe of imperial purple
It speaks
French   "Le Bonheur c 'est le votre—*Compliments!*"
It says before disappearing it isn't
the awaited Representative *Le Bouf Sur Le Toit* of an old friend
                                                    Darius Milhaud

—And yet   O wonder! within the space of an hour   Girls
from the *Face of Enchantment* will again appear on TV today !

NOTE: *Face of Enchantment*: on TV Soap *All My Children*, Suzanne Lucci,
Rebecca Budig, et al.

After Viewing the Motorcycle Diaries
of Che Guevara

At the summer solstice, 20 June, AD 2005

And so it is—*Ainsi*
Today ¡Hoy!
The old man of Earth of myself
gives way to the New Man of Spirit (*Cambio*)   Another
            Change of skin
As Barney dances on the TV screen with
his kid entourage
As a beautiful young woman ties the laces of her running shoes
at the beginning of her day   (to jog
perhaps before going to work)
                              Seeing in the future
Maya my granddaughter twenty years from today
appears at her first one-woman
exhibition at the art gallery
(In New York it is long after Leo Castelli is gone)

I do not know   how
the breach happens How the Moro in me
meets to wed the Byzantine   How my grandmother's smile
found its way
to this New World (the "brave New

World") Miranda intones
in *The Tempest*
After some forty
            or more years   I am still meeting
myself and watching

The extensions of that Self that gathers up
the Araucanias   and the streets of Baghdad   as well

Humid mornings with the smell of Cuban coffee in Havana

And yes, the irresistible cries
of the Sirens

that tormented Captain Odysseos
as his male member became hard and erect
he himself bound
to the mast of his ship . . .
to bypass the inevitable   shipwreck
              naufrage   of the Abyss
Again coming to my lips are the words
دوستیِ من   Dóost-é-mân—Friend ("Che," in the *patois*
of the Argentine
where all roads lead

For Anne (Waldman)

Temoignages—encore

This morning it's still the image   of Prince André
falling off his horse at Austerlitz   Next

Friday's "payday" (for me, *S.S.I.*)   But what good
is it without you in my arms within view of
your fish-net stockings!

                      Comandante CHE's heroic
gigantic photo   looks down
onto the empty street in Havana the while the only two
pedestrians are two fellows who carry a box-spring mattress along the route

—To an unknown destination (¡Adelante!)

I should be asleep   but at this hour
       4:00 a.m. up thinking
of you and where you will be
some ten or twenty years from today

I don't know why that thought comes to mind
but it does

(*l'Afrique*) ancient ruins of *Meroë* the writing remains
still undecipherable wandering shadows

But the Queen of Sheba   left her footprint
there
       (A match for the exposed sole of your own foot
       in the photo)

For Ted Joans

in memoriam

It's   9:16 a.m., July the twenty-fifth
AD 2005

Ted Joans   My Friend

        Is   no longer
    "here"

Nota Bene:
See the Collaboration Poem of S. T. along with Ted Joans, Timothy Baum
(*Nadada*) and Andrei Codrescu-in-Absentia in the volume, *Amtrak Trek*,
New York, 1979, Telephone Books.

The poet, Ted Joans, also associated with French Surrealist poets, friend of
the poet, passed away in Los Angeles, AD 2003. See Ted's *Afrodisia* (1971)
and *A Surrealist Alphabet* (French and English).

Today My Muse Arrived Wearing a Fuchsia Dress

for Antoinette

Today my Muse arrived at my door wearing a fuchsia dress

— —*Toute suite*   presto   *et VOILA!*

I was overwhelmed   She wasn't
in existentialist garb
nor was she going to a funeral in the mode of young punks
                                                    these days

She wore that dress I think for me
            as I was feeling a bit worn from the heat of the day
I don't understand how in the song
it says (the protagonist) "loves"
Paris   "when it sizzles"   "sizzles" should apply
only to eggs and other ingredients in a frying pan
and we weren't
in Paris   She came to my door

                  Just as I was jotting down
the last lines of my poem   Usually we are inclined
to say the Muse arrives *before* we "take pen in hand"
Were she *une jeune Africaine*
she would have been a walking bouquet with shoes to match

The Stranger in the Room

The Stranger in the room, the Stranger who is myself. He watches as I fiddle with papers, toss and turn on the bed, reluctant to get up and sit at my desk and type. The Stranger's in my room with the *maudit* shadow, (*l'ombre*) of the Poe and at the same time frolicsome sun of the "Good Grey Poet" bounding about.

Again, he watches as I expect the beautiful blonde Irina to be standing at my front door out of the blue but she never comes (She's more than likely lost my address some years ago and I am sure her husband Arkadii destroyed my letters to her)

The Stranger in the room sees I've climbed the stairs at least two dozen times today (my room here is at the bottom level and the shared kitchen is upstairs).

The Stranger in the room knows of my resolve not to answer the phone at this time, that is, unless it is a beautiful woman calling and/or an offer of money ("with no strings attached") The Stranger who observes me is in his guise of the *African Prince*
And yes like myself he is nearsighted O Orient O Occident~

Columbus Day of the Year AD 2005

for Fernando Alegria (AD 1920–2005)

In the X or cross of his name
I sit   this day   at my desk
Not knowing how many high-rises or parking towers
have gone up in the last few hours perhaps in New York
or in Kansas? (Except for an error on the map
of Ptolomey these would not have been known)
Or how many of the *indigenous their* names
since eradicated yet remain   (Countess Beatriz

De Boabdilla's face a tantalus for the Admiral's memory)

I too once dreamt of these being lost at sea

But did not know   the motive
or the outcome De La Casas proclaimed (in his books
that were hidden from us then)   O it was the Cities of Gold
of *Cipango*   they were after not the Heavenly City)
Yet out of this error of "the Indies" came

*Romare's   *Black Odysseus*
Pelvic gyrations of Elvis that moved the nations
Alex Haley's finding his way back to *Juffaré*
New Orleans *Blues*   of the "Democratic Vistas"

In the X or cross of his name
I sit this day

NOTES:

In the X of his name. One of early specimens of Columbus's signature,
signed with an X for (Gr.) Cristoforo Fr. Bartolomeo *De Las Casas*
(1484–1566) exposed the brutality of Columbus against the indigenous
peoples of the Americas

*Romare Bearden (*1911–1988*) African American Artist, friend of S. T.

Fernando Alegria, poet, scholar, teacher, Chile, friend of Pablo Neruda and
President Allende, and friend of S. T.

Three Chinese Philosophers

for Jay T. Levine and Calvin Forbes and in memoriam, Ted Joans

"Salut de la démence et libation blême"
  —Mallarmé, *Toast Funebre*
  ([A] pale drink and toast to being crazy)

I've never been   to the moon.
But I saw it once   waiting at the railway station
In Maplewood, New Jersey
It (the moon) didn't have much to say at that moment
Nor did I then for that matter.
I'm happy, though
We are still here three in number
I think
"our number" may be increasing — — ?
By the number of cups of wine we're imbibing
How is this concept "Revolutionary"?
We'll have to write a letter
to *M.* Julian Bond and inquire as to the answer to that question

Ah, it always happens that this particular
"thought" comes along about the thirteenth line

In my dream last evening I was at a conference being courted
by two lovely lady news reporters. Both asked
for my phone number and address.
I can't remember, however, where I was living at the time
But I'd like to get back to that dream.

Anya's Typewriter

for Anya Wozniak-Brayman

There, one slides it in this way . . .. the typewriter ribbon, with the point of a pencil,—no doubt a lost art to this generation so used to using computers, electronic devices (*ordinateurs et Cie.*) But here we've got it,—our new ribbon inserted . . . "ready to go" . . . this gift from our *Bien-aimée* who, out of love, has practically furnished us with a new limb,—this vintage typewriter, this new ribbon upon which to write . . . this the gift *la donnée d' Elle* of Her who is far away . . . she gives us a new limb out of her love

And this limb, a Smith-Corona, upon which she typed her high-school assignments in Syracuse (New York), with all its defects means more to me than any other as my fingertips touch the same keys hers did then, mine join the ghosts of her fingertips at work by the lamp in her room while she was still a schoolgirl, circa 1962, a summer evening
                    or the darkness of a winter night . . .
even in those days when I was unknown to her

the touch of her fingertips across the keys ever conjoined with mine

Seated here before my machine I do not need to drink at the *Fountain of Zem-Zem*, I am already at home at the centre of the world

NOTE: *Fountain of Zem-Zem.* According to Muslim mythology, the fountain's site of the Creation of the world, and its waters contain the elixir of eternal life

"We Were Talking about Octavio Paz ..."

for Sergio Aguilar-Rodriquez and for Ricardo Aguilar-Rodriguez

"A light has gone out",—Well, it was a light we could see with our mortal eyes, anyway, in the moments we have here on this unsettled Planet of ours: a light has gone out, but not really. I mean I always hearken back to that Nahuatl Poet,—*Anonyme*—who said, "The flowers are dying,—what shall we do?" (I don't have the original Nahuatl here before me so we transliterate as best we can. I think here of the poetic sequence of Rene Char as rendered from the French into Italian by the poet, Vittorio Sereni)

As for the politics of the poet, well, you know they are fire—the *gift of fire* given to Man- and Womankind by the Titan, Prometheus. This selfsame fire in the being of the poet, Octavio Paz, which he recognized was in the bosom of all true poets. And, yes, I humbly confess to that same fire burning in me as well, even though I seek for a peaceful glade, as it were, with calm breezes blowing . . .

That same gift of fire *Gramsci* gave us; that Trotsky brought to Mexico (salvaged from the goons of Stalinism in Russia), ignited upon the meeting with André Breton, there at *Coyoácan* (1938)

It is what José Martí called *La hora de los hornos*, that other great Messenger of the fire of Liberation that prophesied *CHE* (Guevara) to us. . . . Do we speak of fire?

In a little church in Chicago, a young woman with her son, *Elvira Arellano*

They have taken refuge there against the monster, *La Migra* here in the United States; do not think they are ever far from me and do you not think I feel their plight every day? And yes their shadows—Elvira Arellano and her young son, Saul,—are everywhere in the rearguard of my poems—and every poet worthy of the name in American at this moment should "Lift Every Voice and Sing" them as a cry to their defense!

Were Octavio Paz here—knowing his politics—I am sure he would raise his voice with mine and cry for *AMNESTY—AMNESTY*,—not only for Elvira and her son but FOR ALL UNDOCUMENTED—so-called "illegal"— IMMIGRANTS in America. But it is enough that you are here and you agree with me, Comrades Sergio and Ricardo Katalina and Marlena (wherever she is at this moment and even if she remembers)

Elvira Arellano and her son, Saul's shadows are cast at this hour!—over every aspect of American life, as they should be.

They haunt the apse of every church and cobwebs in the corners of the White House . . . This mother and her son are the *unseen agenda* at each professor's lectern—no matter what he or she may be lecturing about.

So this is what it all has come to, all this claptrap about democracy and "Freedom" (as always, *whose* freedom: who grants this "freedom" and who are the unlucky ones who are not so recognized?)

Elvira Arellano and her son's name are written in invisible ink on my grocery list as I go out this day; their names are written in the clouds above . . . Mr. and Mrs. John Q. Average American, take their photo from the newspaper, hold it up before you and tell me *What do you see?*

NOTES:

*Anonyme, French, anonymous: reference to the unknown Nahuatl Poet whose works were transcribed in a bilingual version (*Nahua* and Spanish) by the Spanish priest and scholar, Sahagun, in the 16th Century, thirtieth year of the Conquista of Mexco

*Gramsci (1891–1934) *Gramsci*, Antonio, Founder of the Italian Communist Party, imprisoned by Mussolini and died in prison, Rome, 1934. His writings studied by Che Guevara and Fidel Castro, Gramsci's *praxis* Marxism became the foundation of Third World Revolutionary Liberation theory, esp. in Latino-Amer.

Diego Rivera (*1886–1957*) The Mexican artist and revolutionary activist welcomed Leon Trotsky and André Breton to Mexico where in 1938 they jointly wrote and proclaimed *The Manifesto toward a Free and Revolutionary Art*, seeking to revive the spirit of Marxist opposition to Stalinism and "Social Realism" in art.

Hommage to Philip Guston

for Bill Berkson

How or *Why*. Should there be any words at all? *How or Why* should there be any lines drawn on paper, any traces of paint made by the human hand? (True, we have seen some few examples of monkeys and elephants' paintings on exhibit in galleries); but *who* coaxed these creatures into this activity? When did a monkey or an elephant (I admit a love for these creature pachyderms) *conceive* of a painting with a *meaning* or *intention*?). . . .

Dear Philip, these words come too late; I wish I could have evoked them while still in New York way back in 1964, but was fascinated with all painting—the phenomenon thereof . . . starstruck with *Georges Rouault* and at the very end of the spectrum so to speak, the marvels of paint emblazoned on the canvasses of Jackson Pollock—and one who I call a kinsman, *Arshille Gorky*; under the spell of *MARISOL!* (Escovar) and her sculptures . . . Still then a stripling and felt too shy to meet and speak with this gorgeous woman painter/sculptor at Donald Droll's parties; Rauschenberg and his marvel "combines" and the series of "White Paintings"—changed my perspective of the nature of Art (a self-proclaimed French Surrealist I was still infused with the idea of "form"); and Bob Motherwell of course! His series *Homage to the Spanish Republic* still strikes a deep core in me as I see images of the *International Brigades* on parade in Madrid 1938, coming to the aid of the Spanish Republic and its struggle against fascism. . . . Then there were your marvelous covers for Anne's poetry magazine, *THE WORLD,* which even contained my own poems. . . . but by then I was on my way out of New York (end of January, 1967) and *en route* across the country on a Greyhound Bus headed toward the West Coast, to finally "settle"—although I'm not sure that's the appropriate word!—"here", in California (after some forty-four years I'm still not "settled" in this "Golden State," which has quite tarnished in its luster!) my "culture shock" is still an ongoing process here in the Valley of the San Joaquin, maybe a little like Post-Traumatic Stress Disorder to add to my agoraphobic syndrome disorder (which has dogged me since the *Loma Prieta* Earthquake of 1989); raising two daughters here in this State (first celebrated in my book, *The Age of Gold*, KULCHUR, New York, 1976) . . . A continent continues to divide us

Something on TV right now a movie but I'm not really interested in its characters' romantic shenanigans (admit I'd think otherwise if it were Julia Roberts starring in the film).

Earlier I was seated AT my desk. My daughter came into the room and handed me an ad out of a magazine:

I thought of passing that ad on to an elephant.

An American mystic said he once heard of the story of Lao Tzu, the sage is often depicted in Chinese art as astride an ox or a horse seated backwards, letting go of the reins, letting Life take him where it will . . . I look at your paintings, they remind me of that; perhaps why so many poet–friends gravitated toward your work and, though you may have had your own self-doubts, you gave them *so much* for as I see it your paintings and drawings are suffused with the *cri*—the cry—of a poet.

Now even at this late hour, I tell you, your paintings, drawings in particular—all the art you've done—these give me *so much*. Thank You, Friend (though my salute comes to you in absentia) It has taken so long from 1964 to the present for me to find the words to say so . . .

Forty years the Children of Israel wandered in the desert Have I *arrived* to my Canaan-land? Canaan (Arabic, derived from the Language of Aram, *Qenan'iah* لِكَنَائِيَة "Arrived"? (c'est) *arrivée*?

I think always of the line from the film *La Strada* where the character in the guise of a clown declares in a kind of *Absurdiste* pomposity "*Arrivato* Zampano!" (It.) "Zampano's here—*arrived!*" And this Zampano is my Alter Ego, but another *semblable* of myself, semblance of *Godot* (*M*(issing *I*(n) *A*(ction) or the Fool, if you will, The Fool of God (Ramon Lull) . . . *Zen Fool?*—call it what you will

Encompassed in the motto of one of my childhood's favourite characters in the Sunday comics, Smokey Stover's "Notarysojack".

Does time really pass while you are sleeping? Or does Sleep pass when you are timing? *Tempus Fujitsu* occurs when light "strikes the edge of a raindrop and reflects the light"——*Hence*, you are issued a new card with a new identification number that is not, that is not, I repeat, your Social Security Number repeatedly a hit the "delete" key (which shouldn't have to worry either of us, since you are in "a far country"

And I, I am "here" but don't utilise the apparatus anyway

The House of Anne

for Anne Hathaway

Sounds of sand and surf   trails of footprints left
   there to frolic
then intersect   as an X on the beach
of her secret life *Ah Melusine at least you are found again*

And it is here we can define motion again even though
things seem to be "at rest" (thousands
       of years before it was Africa that led to the discovery
of *Relativity*)

Where I find myself again standing where her camels have departed known
as "the event horizon" Manufacturers (*expired*) saving coupons

The inevitable floating plate of burnt toast insinuates

        . . . "Who has said that *becoming*
is a property of beauty"

     Near the half-empty bottle of Dasani
The note reads: "My bright and shining star,
How many times must you be reminded
how beautiful you are?"
In her bedroom near the cheval mirror
     rests the *Diary of a Princess* rests on the top of

the chest of drawers

Apollinaire

Had I the opportunity
I would write his name
in letters taller than
the Empire State Building

Au Rendez-Vous Americain ("XL")

for Lewis Warsh

> *yes   convolute children gamma season*
> *—Joe Ceravolo*

Here we are again   The *40th*
Superbowling "All Singing All Dancing" All boring nabobs
Missed the *Cheerleaders* "halftime" once again the only thing
That makes it all worthwhile   Sometimes   the girls

Of the Shindig dance barefoot on   astroturf
which means   they have only panties on underneath you can't really
"capture" the (American) innuendoes of that
in French; also I must say   in all probability

Not   in Arabic either   (to my knowledge, i.e.,   My ancestral)

Ge'ez   hasn't a word for "panties"   Neither has Grabar
                              (*Ainsi-Soit-Il*) So be it
"We missed each other",   once   remarked
To *Brodsky: "While you were journeying to Auden
and the West I was journeying
              to Mayakovsky and the East"
(He wasn't happy
with that   Nor with much of anything *else*, for that matter

              —"Nuestra arma nuestra palabra"—*Subcomandante*
Insurgent *MARCOS* of Chiapas

The parade of past heroes ("XL") goes on

NOTE: * S. T.'s acquaintance, Russian poet, Joseph *Brodsky (1940–1996)

"Felix Leaves His Imprint Wherever He Goes"

For Antoinette.

-- S., AD2006

FELIX LEAVES HIS IMPRINT WHEREVER HE GOES"

for Antoinette

The Poem Never Saw Daylight

for Adriana Lima of Victoria's Secret

Mon salut un aile clair
—Léopold Sédar Senghor, *Hivernage*

The Poem never saw daylight   (There is always
an interruption quotidian errand upon errand) As it
would ascend but could not approximate   the daylight in your eyes
therein vendagerie of the seas We are always drawn to the abyss

Of your shimmer   which interrogates our foregoing

I hadn't need to open a newspaper this morning

          geography of hunger I know it well familiar to you as the serre
                                        of São Caetano
do Sul the word for history in Arabic *tarikh*   more specific
in meaning than its European counterpart
nor can it sing the bluebird's song for you . . . . . .

                              thus rendered
myself "ineligible"   It is the Poem *imprimes* that now proceeds

As moonlight leaves its Bantustan on your naked shoulder

                    Comprehensive in but one of your glances
O reinvented speech of the child in the *concours* of Salome's veils
As you step forward   (We cannot hope
                              for any better
arrondissement   Vertige   Vertigo

NOTE: * *tarikh*, Arabic,   التاريخ (*l'histoire*)

177

(Actual) Poem Sent to Miss Skala Hassan, of Kurdistan (Iraq), Writing a Dissertation "On Elvis"

The seat at my desk   is like the cockpit of a plane
Each time I ensconce   myself there
(although I have a fear of flying) I meet the Unknown

                    Tom Sawyer's deceptively
painted white running fence still there in
                              (Hannibal, Mo.)

The dialogue between Mar Benjamin Shamoun and Shimko
the Kurd remains   unresolved to this day

                As far as I know, anyway
        I don't share any
genealogical ties with Nebuchadnezzar never having visited
           "Graceland" . . . I would resolve all these differences
if I could in but the wisp of your sable hair
as it blows in the breeze across your forehead
as you stand there speaking to the TV news reporter

           seconds have gone by *Someone's pink hair ribbon*
                floats by in the swimming pool
                      in the apartment complex

Each day is a day of ingenuity

I cook dinner for my daughter as she returns home
        from work
I observe   if anyone will extend courtesy
to me as I'm dressed as a Homeless man crossing the street
             dans ce bois tranquile et sombre
I salute your confidence gracious and luminous
innate powers and strength of Woman
that endure in the world

NOTE: This work was mailed to Miss Skala Hassan at the university where she studies in Kurdistan, Province of Iraq. No reply was received by the poet.

Prolegomena (To Any Future Poetry Prospectus)

for Eleni and Anne (Waldman

There are Greek armies under the sink
no more than an inch tall
I have never tasted
the gourds grown on the moon
Yet the thousand *rubai'ia*
written in praise of your eyes
which I glimpsed for only a moment
have yet to be written

An Heiress

for Paris Hilton

                              As you may have chanced upon
the word   for *Person*   derives from the Latin
Persona   meaning an actor's mask

It's been some eighty-four or more years since
they excavated the tomb of the young African boy

            Pharoah Tutankhamen   (You could

Easily have been the boy-king's consort

Or for that matter, a resident of
Ludwig of Bavaria's castle)

"The Moving Finger   writes"

A malingerer my self when it comes to anything external

to the realm of poetry   My own attribution to longevity
is to follow the dietary regimen of "the oldest woman
in the world", Khfaf Lasuria of Abhazia,—imbibe
            a glass of vodka daily

    But even to take the name of Woman

La Femme   it is your face   reflected in

                The mirror   of Venus   at her toilette
                        by Boucher

When they ask: "Who *are* you, Paris Hilton?"

Mon Ombre Dans le Château

pour Antionette en Vareilles, La Bourgogne, France

De nouveau   de votre anachorète ici

Je ne peut   renverse
le côte   des sphères
celestials   Mes empreintes-des-mains restant dans la penombre
                  d'AXOUM

(C'est l' ame encore   *que montre* le chemin)

Où en
      Harar
où Rimbaud vendrait des fusils

My Shadow in the Château

for Antoinette at Vareilles, Burgundy, France

Again   From your anchorite   here

I can't reverse
the direction   of "heavenly
bodies"   My handprints remain in the penumbra
                                    of *A X U M*

(It is the soul   that goes its way)

Or   in
            Harar
where Rimbaud   sold guns

Saroyan's Oracle, "No Foundation . . ..!"

IT WAS in 1976, on the occasion of an address given before one of my Readings in San Francisco,—I have forgotten where it was—that I paid homage to an old friend, William Saroyan, citing a line from one of his most noted plays, *The Time of Your Life*. It is spoken—almost chanted through the scenario of the play, which takes place in a barroom as the patrons there converse on the "ups and downs" of life, speculating on their own fate and the fates of others. The line has haunted me these thirty years and I cite it here and now. It is spoken by a wispy character in the play, called "The Arab", who obsessively paces up and down the bar-room floor, his only words being these:

"No Foundation up and down the line, no Foundation!" . . ..

These are the only words The Arab utters throughout the course of the play, seemingly oblivious to the other characters' attempts to draw his attention to their intense discussion the whys and wherefores of life as we know it. The Arab goes on with his peripatetic antiphon:

"No Foundation up and down the line, no Foundation!"

This nameless Arab is like a one-man Greek Chorus whose chant restates the basic absurdity of human life. For me this one line is *plein de poésie*, an anticipation even of Beckett's *Godot*, or one of the character out of Jarry's *Ubu Roi*, itself a prefigurement of French Surrealism.

"No Foundation, up and down the line, no Foundation!"

Most poetic and at once most poignantly philosophical lines in my estimation in all of literature. I say that in thirty years these words of Saroyan's Arab are an insight into the workings of modern-day existence, I should say, rather, *American life*—after all, the play doesn't take place in Paris but in San Francisco! This eschatological madman—successor to Nietzsche's Madman—this Arab's words *resonate* down to our own time, the Era of Technology, so-called.—A succinct jeremiad of contemporary American life,—a society withal its contradictions that has become or is on its way to becoming a virtual nightmare: from the puppet shows on TV with "live" people the media puts on for us; the Bush "Neocon" Whitehouse with its news conferences where everyone languidly applauds the chief of state as he enters the room; to advertisements about drugs—commercials—that promise to "unblock" arteries, lower cholesterol or enhance one's sexual performance; matchmaking by computer to meet one's ideal mate in lieu of actually going out to take the "risk" to meet someone *live*; and of course the telephone answering system that constantly warns us with its preamble, "Listen carefully, as the Menu has changed"—"*Changed?*" *Changed* to *what?*

Who're you kidding? Sorry, my British friends, the foregoing is an "Americanism", many of which I am guilty of in my speech, without knowing how better to express myself . . . "Who're you kidding?" How to translate that into "proper" English—yet another of my perpetual problems with that bug-a-boo, *Language!* As Sweeny Agonistes says in *The Wasteland* of Mr. Eliot, "I gotta use words when I talk to you", yet another sibylline utterance for the "New World Order" of our day. Well, we can possibly render it this why, "With whom are you playing Blind-Man's Bluff—?" But let us return to the Arab's oracle:

"No Foundation up and down the line, no Foundation! . . . "

Now we might think this Arab is something of an Existentialist. He indicts Western Civilisation but has nothing in common with the ilk of Osama bin Laden and his cohort of Islamicist nuts who have vowed to destroy America and the West they condemn as "unbelievers" (a hateful distortion of Islam) . . . .. Now I don't know if Saroyan's Arab in *The Time of Your Life* is a Marxist, as Marx's message might be interpreted as this same "No Foundation" to our *hubris*, our "Globalisation",—the answer to the gentleman who in the movie *Wall Street, exclaims, "Greed is *good!*"

But the Marx of the *Grundrisse* surely must have *something* in common with this absurdist peripatetic Arab of *The Time of Your Life*. I think of him also a little like *Marcel Marceau*—that supreme mime of our time: except this mime *speaks*, even if he has these few words to give and then vanish into oblivion.

I know for sure the character of The Arab is a poet.

He remains the eternal oppositionist, *a shadow of myself.*

NOTE: * Wall Street: Gordon Gecko

Étonnement May 15th

for Amber Tamblyn

It is 9:30 a.m. I am cooking broccoli. It is already unbearably hot. Beethoven *Symphony No. 1* on radio. A house painter passes by peering at the open door—mine—perhaps wondering what is the strange music and the even stranger denizen who dwells in this apartment. Somewhere a woman is dying her story being captured on video for a wide audience.

What would we do—what could we possibly have done—without the existence of a *Beethoven—it is unimaginable! If there never had been a God-sent saviour if not of the whole human race then at least the saviour of my own individual *sanity* living here!

Haven't seen an *Efik* mask in ages (their art seems to resemble that of the South Seas, Melanisia, in effect.

I guess it's yet again Parmenides versus Heraclitus: Action verses Contemplation (the immobile, unchanging. Being, of Parmenides whereas with the Ionian philosopher it is change that is at the centre of things: "even the gods change") in this interim *where am I?*

The *Mobilgas* sign at the garage I used to espy out of the car window in my boyhood while out for a drive with my father, the red Pegasus emblem the name of which I didn't as yet know but which would be a portent other than the brute smell of petrol spilled on tarmac an inclination somehow of a meeting between heaven and earth augured for me in that winged creature.

In a momentary flash a cockroach rears its ugly head to make an about-face at the corner of one of my manuscript boxes perhaps something the Bard of Avon himself might have glimpsed on one of his wakeful nights?

And nearby as I write your photo in the guise of *Joan of Arcadia* sent to me when you were but sixteen years of age still captures your allure (my rapturous letter sent to you however went unanswered

NOTE: * As regards Beethoven, I could have as well said the same about Mozart,—or BACH, Vivaldi, Corelli,—Or Tchaikovsky! Prometheus, it is said, stole fire from the gods to bring it to Man- and Womankind: so the composer plucks from the empyrean to make music the intermediary between heaven and earth

perhaps on the advice of your publicist at the time, given the fact of the recent "stalking" of stars of TV by crazed fans.)

Several days have passed.

Still haven't obtained any further information on the *Efik* people but retain in my memory the marvel of their masks (the book in which these were featured has long since been lost) but I am not charged here with conveying any anthropological information in general it is solely the *art* of those mysterious people with which I am concerned.

(**Efik*, a tribe of South Eastern Nigeria, related to the *Ibio* ethnic group of that nation.)

8:41 a.m. here.   5:41 p.m. in Piccadilly Circus

I see at the moment there isn't any tea yet brewing on the stove.

O sviluppo artritico   (My tongue remains the pen of a ready writer *Psalmos 45*) "What is life?" writes the Russian mystic, Skovoroda, "It seems (to be) a Journey; well, then, I am on it; nonetheless I know not where I am going or why." In the same spirit Breton speaks with his first words in *Nadja* — — and the fount from which all the words of my life have been drawn and still continue to emanate and assemble.

A Lady's Eyelash Circled the Number (117) on the Page of the Book . . .

It appeared blonde and of course immediately

I thought of who *she* was

Perhaps a girl of twenty How long ago
had the fallen lash been left there   A generation
or two?

Had she taken the book with her on vacation
perhaps to Bordeaux
Or read it lounging naked, lithe limbs

stretched on the beach at Antibes or at Marrakech
                    (Was it then still France *Outre Mer*)?

It came as always unannounced, when there's
not a bit of notebook paper near
As again I realize I've missed the price of gold
on the Market today   And again what good
would it do me anyway?

Where did she pause to espy her image on what show window as she passed
by and *pli-éd*

5:30 melancholy (brûler l') *étape*, i.e., atoll at my fingertips
As I turn the page to look upon it once more
the eyelash's vanished

Dans le Château de Vareilles, Autun, France

(Feuilles) pour Antoinette en vacance en Autun

Couleurs de le spectre ici dans ma main, ce petit cristal rayonnant de violet du quartz (de quelque caverne *Aurignacien* se refleter à travers la nuit vers a moi?)

À le trois heures au matin   Vous s'éveiller

Mon lit (ici) voici comme le sable blanc du Sahara
          (Ah, *présence Africaine* encore dans ma sang)
déjà   desolée sans toi   Ma mémoire c'est comme

     Une Minotaure qui dévorer les événemnts de la jour passé
     Eh!—Voila le siècle minotaurien de Picasso l'artiste se concevoir de même comme une bête (l'implication peut-être, de l'éroticisme du peintre *lui même!*)
     Et moi,—j'ai l'affliction du Langage! que *m'épreuve tous les jours* . . . (Malraux l'écrit *l'Antimémoires*) (une de mes livres perdus Maintenant
          —*Moi* qu'est *l'Homme Perdu*)
     Tes belles épaules teint de bronzé où je l'ai mis une baiser fugitif pas plus tard qu'hier

NOTE: *Minotaure: (Le Minotaure et sa labyrinthe)* Bête mytho-logique, moitié homme et moitié taureau, desseinée par Daedelus pour le roi Minos dans l'île de Crète.

The Castle of Vareilles, Autun, France

for Antoinette

Colours of the spectrum radiate here in my hand, this small crystal radiates violet from its quartz (from some Aurignacien cave its reflections traverse the night to me?)

3 o'clock in the morning   You're awake

My bed like the white sands of the Sahara
                (Ah, Africa's *présence* in my blood)
already desolate   without you   My memory is that

        Minotaur that devours the events of the passing day
    And here the series of the *Minotaur* of Picasso the artist conceives of himself thus as a beast (the implication being that of the painter's own eroticism!)

    As for myself—the affliction of Language continues day after day . . .
(Malraux wrote *Antimemoires*) (one of my lost books)   Even so
        it is I (who am lost), "*The Lost Man*"

    Your exquisite bronze-tinged shoulders upon which I placed a fugitive kiss (it seemed) only yesterday

NOTE: *The Minotaur* (and its *labyrinth*) mytho-logical beast half man half bull created by Daedelus for king Minos of the Isle of Crete.

For Antoinette at the Castle of Vareilles

Pèlerinage

I.

   "To be human", then. Is not simply to be defined as an "upright featherless biped", but to recognize that as a human one has a "past" and a "future"; and that this tension between arises like a sea squall in the present creates *angst* or anxiety (Which is something Plato had neglected in his analogy demarcating the human from the animal world. I know of no scientist yet who has probed the animal mind to find there an anxiety about the "future"!)

   To be human—deserves justice and *right (le droit)*: habitation for the race to perpetuate. Shelter that will not only protect from the elements *but allow also for the perpetuation of wonder,* of the creative spark

                                                                (At the moment I
          listen to the *Concerto for Harp* of Germaine Taillefer: I propose it
          could not have been composed if its creator were left to the
          exposed unbearable heat and sand-storms of the Sahara; some
          suitable humane shelter would have had to be afforded to the artist
   so *that she could* create her masterpiece in peace, given only to the rise and
   fall of the tempest perhaps of the spirit's own ebb and flow within

2.

   Recalling the philosopher, Gabriel Marcel's view of the human enterprise, its state of "brokeness", "man . . . becoming aware of his condition as a traveller" . . .. that it may be that "the whole question is to know whether in *refusing* to make this venture" that is that of the *Homo Viator*, or human wayfaring itself in the world) "We are not starting on a road which sooner or later may ultimately lead to perdition"

Nota Bene: Monsieur Gabriel Marcel wrote these emblematic words in 1943, that most bleak of years, in Occupied Paris, with his whole nation in a state of collapse and under the noxious rule of the Vichy government of Pétain. I say these words are duly applicable today, in AD 2006, when the whole world is in a state of collapse.

"The View from Bedford Falls"

for Donna Reed (1921–1986), Actress, (It's a Wonderful Life)

This phrase came into my head today. Don't know where I'll go with it. It's a substrata of "It's a Wonderful Life" (*George Bailey & Co.*) with a rather macabre time setting of *AD 2007*. (I don't know the particular significance of that either.)

"The View From Bedford Falls" . . .

The fish named "Blue" is now awake. Everyone else in the house apparently still asleep I can roam around The feared dictator meets the revered but klutzy president in heaven (both having exited this life at the same hour)

"What did you *do?*" asks the president.

"I killed millions of people and maintained my power by ruthless yet efficient means. And what did *you* do, Mr. President?"

"Er, I tripped a lot; shot some good games of golf. I believe I helped ease some of the anxiety of a nation; brought about some healing for those who felt betrayed, that is, not to say that betrayal would not again follow . . ."

And so

the two shades join hands in journeying
the ellipsis of the empyrean realm . . . .

—The telephone rings suddenly (*Poof!* there goes *that*) . . . . a cell phone—7 a.m. with no one up to answer
It takes a year and a day before the water heats to
cook a hard-boiled egg   As I'm seated here alone in this
kitchen next to my granddaughter's "Easy Bake Oven", longing
for a dream-girl *Playmate* in a bikini

The egg   does its final dance
in the boiling pot of water. The hippopotamus upstairs prepares to go to
work. Soon he'll be seen getting into his compact car parked in the driveway
(as usual blocking my daughter's car (there is no garage in this house.)

Hello. I hear human breathing in the bathroom.

It would be a bit more daunting if I told you I hear animal breathing
there in the stalls possibly that of a hairy mammoth But no as I venture a

look there's no one there but myself. *Quelqu' un c'est ET NON est une fantôme?*
Susa   (la Cité) Sît Shámsi, modèle votif de le Soleil au Levant   12 e Cen. (*Paris Musée de Louvre*)—*Ishtar*! Do you still search for your *Tammuz?*

On the walk
The child striding past with her mom smiles at me, perhaps because she has not seen such a creature before *en Amerique*
                    Hélas Ils sont chinoises   la mère et sa
                                                              jeune fille

    Au lever du rideau
c'est toujours   —Doudoù debout Doudoù

Wanted to stage Aristophanes's play *The Clouds* in a bowling alley but they wouldn't let me

FROM JOE CERAVOLO: (1968)
JOE'S LETTER—ILLUSTRATION IN 3 PAGES

en souvient mon ami
Joe (Ceravolo)
c. 1967.

⑦

" stay home &

⑤
③

⑧

If you decided on applying
for a grant and I ~~had~~ received one,
you could use me as a
recommendation. You have
much, mucho, talent and
there's no saying how deep
you could go. America needs you!
Love from Rosemary over to
all three of you.

Love from *Paul and Cerita
(I's children)
(I'm sure)
** to Tatyana
*Tatyana
(my 1st child,
then 6 mos.
old. (b. 5/4/62
in San Jose, Cal.)

Love from me
Joe

195

To Joe Ceravolo
"Frenzy of Madmen Ecstasy of Saints"

> *Au terme d'un long voyage*
> —Paul Éluard

I have traveled the expanse of the Gobi

Left my castle in air   for the struggles
                                        of Earth

I have been led to learn diverse languages of the world
    that I might learn to communicate with your own speech
The trees   even the leaves themselves
in the Silence   have been my teachers   even as the rushing waters

Paintings of artists come alive for me so that I could see you anew

                        An Exile I have followed the Cloud by day
                and Pillar of Fire by night
have observed the extremities
of human darkness and its moments of light

            naufragés   (shipwrecks)   storms and halcyons

And yet have been able   to transcend these

Measurements
of scientists I have found insufficient

            To realize the expanse of the soul

Which rivals the marvels of Luxor
                        or the treasures of Florence of
                                        the Renaissance
glories contained in the Louvre in Paris itself

And yes wounds
have been my traveling companions
as guides (as were yours)
to point the way beyond
myself
to the Marvellous   they have built monuments
                                        out of misfortune

The uncharted route of this journey
and the greatest of marvels   has placed me
suddenly in your domaine my *amanecer Mon Aube* (My Dawn

Nuncio without Portfolio from Kush

for the birthday of Antoinette, 5 February, AD 2007

"I'm on it rightaway", that is, your *birthday*
I wear no war paint today
I have no Black Hills of the Dakotas as my background
I almost forgot! (as is my wont these days
   between avalanches
      of books and papers in my room)
A Chorus waits in the wings *of more than a billion words of*
The Oxford English Dictionary now
tuning up
to serenade you (Unfortunately, you don't have a balcony
 available) like Juliet to stand on barefoot
But that can be forgiven I'll take
you in the sheerest lingerie
standing at your front door
at six in the morning any day
calling out to "Missy" and "Georgie"
your two *bichôn-frise* to "hurry up" and *do* their "stuff"

  As you wait there (legère)
as a goddess come to life out of Phidias's Athenian marble

NOTE: Kush, or Cush, Ancient African Kingdom, now vanished
in the region of Nubia.

198

For Ramona Akl Somewhere in Caracas

Somewhere   in Caracas
You awaken with

That svelte yawn of yours pink rooftops
of the city There aren't any Italian poets of the *Trecento*
to serenade you

      With madrigals

           your eyes ever invoke
    the *oud* عُوْدٌ

     Its music removes
even further from you now

With the name   *Ramallah*

              And your ancestors'
Arabic   become remoter
Although I hear its plaintive   syllables
still sing

In your blood as much as in mine

As in the Odes inscribed in *Thuluth*

              calligraphy
on the interior of the walls of Alhambra
in Granada

Letter to a Lady Astronaut

to Lisa Nowak

I admit to still being haunted by the undulation of Marlene Dietrich's legs
Very often the pot in which I cook spaghetti boils over
That is when I happen to be lying down engrossed in reading the comics
of the Sunday paper, *Garfield* and *Sally Forth* and treating myself to a
gargantuan chocolate-chip cookie along with my morning cup of coffee
I use the cuneiform tablet on my desk as a paperweight
Am also "reminded" of how far we have come,—from fooldom to (male)
fooldom   which claims the name of "human civilization"
Admitting there *are* exceptions, however   Election of Chilé's first
Woman President, *Mme. Michelle Bachelet,* who honors her forebear, the late
President Salvador Allende (I keep her name by the side of my typewriter as
a sign of *Hope—l Espoir*—for this so-called anthropoid charade of ours
But you must be dizzy from a flight beyond the speed of sound

À La Mère de Ma Muse

à Mme. Angelina Médearis

There are birds there playing in the fountain   They
don't know your name
But I do   (Well, parenthetically)
because of your daughter the woman I love
No I am not
from the planète Mars   I take up
my residence here on *La Terre si vous plait*
(that is, Earth) (Here a fanfare!)
                    It's truly for
            the moment anyway a Spring morning I still
don't understand the Californians
seated here on an outdoor bench furnished for the

Pedestrian by the local Realty Co. I'm not ready to
buy a house just yet Thank You (until an endless windfall of 1000 dollar
bills comes my way)

I'm assailed
by poetry every minute of the day I can't hide fast
enough to   "throw it off the trail"

There's still a Château waiting in Auteil

As you will see from my photo (which is absent)
I am not *Rasputin*   The Americans remain
devoid of manners all drum majors cries une Voix the Voice
                      in the desert of myself

Days of Max's Kansas City

for Bill Berkson and for Shelley Scott-Lustig

The procession of artists and their entourages must still
be going on guys with sinkfulls of flowers on their heads
women dragging along their flat tires from their Bugattis
the din rising promptly   at about 8 p.m.   and then
a crescendo   at 9 p.m.   maybe at that time Frank Lima
might have made an entrance (or thought better of it)
in Hamletic pants wearing a ten-gallon hat the "size of
Texas"   Even though Larry Rivers is gone and girls have
now taken to smoking cigars   (to prove *what?*
   well to look *chic*   saveurs of Bon Jovi (pseudonym
of *Bon Ami*) As day   follows night as surely as
my Arabic ancestors Ethiopians and Armenians improved upon
the *Stagirite's logic   and I can't glean a bit of it but no loss
it makes a pretty design   on the page   where Moss Hart takes
a bow minus punch-line confettis
   all appears like the siege of an ancient castle the lines
slowly making their way sorry no conga line up to the finish
line of the bar mirrors and chrome stools   eskimos penguins
Rockefellers albatrosses latrines Cinderellas latest starlets
from *Pixar's Folly* Now that I've got everything and everyone
all on one harness I do
   miss my early morning conversations at Mary's Café with
painter Nate Oliveira in the days when I actually could
afford to buy the "breakfast special" (minus the meat
Thank You) It's true we never arrived   at the "Unanswered
Question"   What Is   Art (?) I'm sure Tolstoy must have
had a bad taste in his mouth in attempting *that one* or maybe too
much absinthe instead of *Smirnoff?* (As *it is written*
the "size of a man's moustache mustn't exceed the size
of his eyebrows"

Note for Andy and Rose in Paris
at the Summer Solstice

for Andrew and Rose Joron

Ce qui frappe surtout dans ces belles forêts du détroit
                    —Dénis Roche
(What's even more striking in the midst of
these lovely forests of the straits)

Where you wander the streets of *La Cité*

                              Nietzsche's Madman again cries
O dust of *Jocko*, The Elephant shot
for meat during the last days of *The Commune*
Mummies hidden beneath the streets of Paris
a fallen star   *(étoile d')*   there

Staggers on the *Champs Elysées*
as it lifts itself up and dusts cosmic dust from
        its tuxedo lapels
aided by my marsupial shadow
Look
inside
the heel of your wife's shoe there
are rose buds there

Paris Hilton

I maintain.   The state of the Alphabet
remains the same   it's a minute past ten
And Archimedes's claim
"Give me a lever and a proper place to stand
and with it I shall move the world"

Someone's wiggling
their toes at this very moment   *in Paris*
(Could very well have been South Dakota) I haven't as yet
inquired about the state of economy this morning
In East Africa the sale of two cattle I believe still

Buys a wife for a fellow (and possibly some accoutrements
along the way) I am happy you're not veiled
and strolling about like a walking circus tent But your smile
                                    returns me to Mallarmé's *Au Délà*
that immediacy O Mulier amicta "clothed with the sun"

I'm often tired after writing a poem and lie down with
no *hetaire* here to soothe me but photos
next to my bed   Princess Di and Lee Radziwill (circa 1970 taken
by Andy Warhol) yours as well there
Woman's Beauty as ever illuminates the world.

NOTE: *Mulier amicta* sole et luna sub pedibus ejus, Apocalypse 12.1

Letter to a Turkish Writer M. Orhan Pamuk, Winner of the Nobel Prize for Literature, AD 2007

for Khatchik Minashian, Ashough, and for Charlie Rose.

Dear Sir: In your interview you speak about the primacy of Craft. *Craft?* Ah, Craft-man-ship, you say? How does a man then *craft* craft a ship? Why not a Womanshipcraft? Or craft-ship-man? ORHAN POMUK, cows craft milk in their bellies chimneys craft smoke in their fireplaces. Donald Duck crafts *quack-quacks* in his quackery CRAFT of *Yea* and *Nay* Kraft of cream-cheese Kraft of Frederick the Great who composed ditties to amuse himself whilst observing battles in which men were slaughtered (we have, therefore, the *I.Q.* and the craft of Frederick the Great Thinker and Musician) *Craft,* you say craft you say Say your craft sail your craft upon what Sea *See?*
As for craft:
    Nota Bene: 6 Million Armenians cry out in me
    An untold number of Africans kidnapped by White Slavers from their respective
        homelands *en Afrique* sold into Slavery by *your muslim craftsmen* cohorts cry out
      in me Cyprus cries out in me—to be rid of the craft of Turk occupiers

The streets of Paris are paved in craft but my merest of lines are more important than these "All roads lead to Rome" it was once said; but *all roads lead to *VAN!—Lake Van*—and *there's* where you can dip your pen in its *bloodred ink* of the Nameless Ones who perished in 1915 Ottoman glory (That same glory that butchered men women and children who took refuge within the sanctuary of Hagia Sophia in 1453 in Constantinople) *Craftmanship?* Graftmanship of my grandmother's brocade black red and gold of the Island of Sicily! Lepanto!
—ORHAN POMUK! I fell asleep listening to your words during your TV interview tonight but the ages they were wide awake and they laughed with the stars in the fertile night where the paintings of Arshille Gorky bear witness ever burning brightly to light the way

NOTE: *Van, site of the *preëminent genocide* of the Twentieth Century— slaughter of 6 million Armenians on the death march by Turks, 1915. Many of these are Nameless Ones, recalled only by oracular family histories. *To its eternal dishonour, the Turkish Nation* refuses to acknowledge this crime.

Aujourd'hui

À Mlle Noélle Oxenhandler et pour Max Jacob

Aujourd'hui   je suis chinois   c'est-à-dire

                   en ce moment seulment

comme Lao-Tzé   ou comme Li-Pô

j'avais aussi   un peu   de lune réfléchi dans

un petit ruisseau   un peu de herbe   dans le chemin

              les nuages hospitaliers

Voici mon vin   (est) rouge et frais

(Pendant que ma chat regarda

les voisins entrants et le sortants)

Je cuisinier spaghetti

Je me plier mes pantalons   (légitiment)

         Je l'invente le pays

            du Bordeaux

Je parle anglais Je m'appele Harmâttan un peu vertigineux

Je vous dis   *Bienvenu*   à mon château de carton

C'est vrai qu'on connait bien peu ceux

qu'on aime Maintenant c'est bien Je me danser avec les silhouettes

des mes amours perdus   encore l'ange du

rose-blanche dans votre front *Circassièn*   s'annoncer

          (de ce spectacle la miênne)

"Dépêchez-vous

    —Il partira immédiatement!"

Today

(Translated from the French of the Author)
for Mlle. Noëlle Oxenhandler (and for Max Jacob

Today   I'm Chinese   that is to say
                    in this moment only
Like Lao Tzu   or like Li-Po
I have a bit of moon reflected in
a brook a bit of green along the way

          The hospitaler clouds
      Here's my wine a refreshing red
(As my cat looks out the window
at my neighbors' coming and going
I cook spaghetti
(ah,) I've split my pants   (truly)
         I've invented   the land
                     of Bordeaux
I speak English   I'm called *Harmattan*   a little dizzying
I bid you good day   from my cardboard CHÂTEAU
It's true we know little of
those we love However it's O.K. I dance with shadows
of my past loves   Yet the white-rose angel
of your Circassian brow   Announces
                (this is my spectacle)
       "Better hurry
     It's leaving soon!"

Coming to Meet You at the Summit

for Courtney Lehmann

I'm not being carried supine on a litter
by elliptical Nubians
      Nor on a troop ship bound for
                      Illium
            At the moment
I can't quite reach the "remote" while speaking to you
    on the phone   Your voice is the *Lido*
I'm still missing
      all the castles in Spain
But not a bottle of champagne, which for the first time
being must remain invisible

    But here's a spare mermaid
        who'd be happy to swim
            with you in your pool
   (I'd love to, too, but I can't swim!)

The "original" Harlem Globetrotters dance and "dribble"
   heralds of Africa's majesty We mustn't forget, however,
Queen Maeb's   train of "little atomies launched
    from a parson's nose"
                      —continues
our project to create and—re-create ourselves
    and our world

"I'm at Page 61 Now ..."

for Dale Smith

I'm at page 61 now
Of the *Black Stone* "Great Read", as they say
But still don't know what
the stone is maybe it's that
Ding-an-Sich
that *Chinaman of Koenigsberg spoke about
Maybe a delicate almost undecipherable
mole on a girl's leg (which you wouldn't
necessarily see unless you undressed her / age 21)

Might be Vanessa Redgrave's *Fever* her
Life force rivets when she turns
her gaze to you   I'm supposed to be

Asleep now 1 a.m. (enterprising adept of St. Pol Roux's
                                        oneiric workshop)

I've never learned the secret
of the African's talking drums even though
the code's in my blood the *Siné-Salôum*

Or Odysseo's   "OÚJ∫S"?   even rows of yellow flowers
that illumine the streets of the *Café Flore* now as she
walks by so regally I have forgotten
the name of the flowers

NOTE: *Immanuel Kant (1724–1804), German philosopher, postulated the Ding an Sich, the "thing in itself", in his philosophy.

Another "Very Good Week" on Wall Street

Another "very good week" on Wall Street
And a man
crawling "on all fours" in the Mission
District, San Francisco   (This did not happen
before my eyes, but it was reported)
And coaldust on the faces of the miners who
   have come up unrecognizable out of the hole in the earth
that their faces as blackface the vaudeville comedians once wore
Record number of homes   Up   For Sale   owners
having "defaulted" on mortgages All the while
I wanted very much to have Scheherezad in my embrace she appeared

However on my walk this morning in the guise of a bent
woman in her 84th year she told me
the doctor advised her *not* to dine on vegetables but only "meat"
How's that for a theme for you young poets
I must confess, however
I really wasn't very
"inspired" today (You were
asking "How *was* it"?)
A very good week

Cada Día Para Mi Compañero Ernesto Cardenal

Each morning at first light I wait   *amanecer*
I wait for the words
      (in French, *Les Mots,* in Spanish, *Las Palabras,*
          Arabic كلمة

    I wait for the words to come
I know I am but the door for
    their entry or *re-entry* into the world
But without them I remain barren
I am like the prophet *Jeremias*
cast into the pit

(8:45 a.m. More than an hour has flown) outside the city limits
the Migrants must be having some semblance
of breakfast about now and waiting, too

On streetcorners Jalisco Michoácan Zacatecas Guerrero Yucatan
A guitar takes wing and flies
          into the heavens minus its human owner
to bring some music to the besieged
A *Victoria's Secret* model steps out of the pages
of the catalogue to model for me her latest lingerie   But she
Disappears in the moment I try to grasp her
reliving again the story of Orfeo and Eurydice

    Here is the word   *Le Monde*   *El Mundo*
(along with a floodgate of words) written   *Rocio*

   Now where she is   like her name
           dew of the dawn

On Aaron Copeland's Birthday

November 14th, AD 2007
for John Ashbery

Unlike the tribe of "thinkers"
the imagination responds   to the word, "angel". At least
we still have with us such grand Archetypes and splendours
for Americans to ponder, who've grown cynical
about "foreign aid" (a dark day Christmas, 1958, in São Paolo
      your *Fanfare,* for those who dwelt
like Carolina Maria—and still dwell in favelas)

Ah Laura Ingraham and the Republican National Committee!
I mean you no harm (*!no falta!*) but consider
that for your WASP hauteur I don't know where "we"

Go from "here" as still can't read (other than the *clef*
a note of music on the page   But can serve
breakfast in bed to the woman I love who happens to be
in absentia this morning I can't believe it's already 6:43 a.m.
and this is all I've come up with   *Cher ami*
Si je gagnais   *le premier prix du Loterie*

Here's the travesty of my age-
ridden visage in the mirror   I celebrate and set aside
November 14th as my own holiday

(From the) Dust of Balzac

Hoofbeats of Agincourt on a plush rug parlour
somewhere in Paris make me want to write again
after having quit it for the umpteenth time Here the fools
barbecue that's all they do it seems to mark the Summer
L'Été
      And indeed had I quit only the madhouse would await
my being fitted for one of its jumpsuits a thrust as it
is said Sappho the poet did and to think *had it been* had it been the sea
that swallowed up those pitiful boats Niña Pinta and Santa
Maria instead of spewing them out onto the shores of the "New World"
            that would have cancelled my meeting with the bishop
on Tuesday cancelled the head of a numbskull Fraternity
Society from becoming "President" and yes it would have
cancelled the swaying back and forth of those trees I see
through the window but what is most hurtful of all it
would have   ANNUL-EE   CANCELLED

My conversation with you this afternoon over the telephone

      Yet Shostakovich would still be there and Ida and
Ani Kavafian rendering the composer on the violin
where an angel would be trying to balance on the bowtip
continuously losing its balance with each slide again and
and *Oops*

Pancakes and Champagne for Breakfast

for Michelle Kosinsky

le vivace et le Bel Aujourd'hui
—Mallarmé

Having heard of the subject from a distance
decided an interview would be in order I don't know
if any tickets are extant from the overflow of passengers on the Arc
(now docked in drybed, or so they say, on Mt. Ararat)
In the morning to start things off so to speak
I rub my bald pate like a crystal ball (It
works!) may be a bit "dated"
but here's some ticker tape coming out
my left ear As I was saying the great disadvantage of the modern
man's dress shirt is that it's without a pocket
thence when you go to grasp for a pen there's
nothing there but air!   Geronimo
never had to worry about that, except in
his last days when he signed autographs for fans while
motoring about in his Model *T* Inexplicable sister
of the Minotaur enigma and masque As you're just in from Dakar
To catch you in an embrace as you drop
your trench coat It was a "last minute" decision
to expand the lines of the poem to go off
the page just this once

Today I Wear My Oleg Cassini Tie . . .

for Bill Berkson and Connie Llewelen

Alors aujourd'hui. . . .

Today I wear my Oleg Cassini tie (It happens
to be a Sunday) This isn't
the "room of genius"
but it is the place
where from some mysterious source
Poetry flows (I could easily say
Poetry flows from my Oleg Cassini tie
                    between its silk silver and
          sepia stripes

But who would believe it, much less
see it!)

I hope the elephants in Africa are happy

now at this moment, in knowing
their ivory tusks (*défense d'ivoire*) are
at last protected I still retain a memory
of the towers of Manhattan, especially

Lita and Bear's 13th Floor of the Penthouse
888 Park Avenue where I could look out
on the world
My "dry" (Vodka not gin) Martini sits majestically on
the kitchen counter (minus its olive 8:45 a.m.
ready to sing an aria or *arioso*

Wandered long thirsty in a dry land to find
the Spring

Against "National Poetry Month"

for Garrett Caples and Anna Naruta

"la poésie est inadmissible"
—Dénis Roche

It was from the spilled blood of Medusa
that Pegasus sprang forth and took wing   from there
that blood stained the margins
of the blank page of Mallarmé
light waves move through the "ether" just
as sound waves move through air   (But, then
    they have come to question if ether even exists)

The battlements of Elsinore I find
at every corner I battle Tilamât
I hear the moans of those along the endless march
   of Van prodded by bayonets (Ottoman Turk
murderers' perfected elegance of the *Ghazal*)

*Harar ever calls   out within me even though
I do not journey there, preferring the few luminous
strands of hair left by the loved one on my bed (*l'Absente*) to carry
me through the ennui of day and night and the void
        (*Le Vide*)   Yes, keep
notebooks and pens handy for the soul's folly (As my dress
shirt hangs in the bathroom to dry)
And the murderers continue to poeticize and protect their borders

NOTES:

Tilamât, ancient Babylonian monster-god of Chaos who fought Marduk.

Van, site (now in Turkey) of the Death March, genocide of millions of Armenian men women and children, 1915. Preeminent genocide of the Twentieth century intimating the Holocaust.

l'Absente, that is to say, The Absent Woman (lover)

Harar, loc. N. Ethiopia. The last adventure of poet Arthur Rimbaud as merchant and gun-runner to King Menelik of Ethiopia, (1880s).

When Vanna (White) Says "Bye!"
on TV's *Wheel of Fortune*

When *Vanna* (White) says "Bye!" on TV's *Wheel (of Fortune*
I think of the addresses I've lost or which
I can't locate at the moment I'll have need of them. The Sea
of Tranquility signals it will flower occasionally white or pink
instead of red
The golden apple thrust by Paris in the Three Goddesses' midst
continues to roll on   beyond
their grasp   It may be immediately apparent
but this is as much a Manifesto as any

Of the other writings "Not too great
a leap of faith", so to speak   sensations
of hunger and thirst transmitted through the brain
"Two contradictory pictures of 'reality'" then unfold neither of which fully
explains the phenomenon of light

The modern technological cyclops wags its shimmy-dance
Africa still   in the throes of waking (dawn on the Serengeti Plain)

So the day ends My Lady with its *éclarissement*
in your shimmer

A Woman's Cough Heard (Approx. 9:40 p.m.)

for Bob Rauschenberg (1926–2008)

Location—? —Outside in the veranda—momentary
      (no description of the woman, as she
      wasn't visible to me) We can assume, however

It may possibly have been
a blonde, demure cough?

Watching my shadow flutter against the far wall there
it seemed by candlelight, but it was really
the night-light.

The Knight's Vision by Raphael comes immediately to mind
                    I don't know
what provoked it,   as
clatter from the neighbour's telly upstairs rolled on
in the interstice. And here, I admit
as a character actor reading from a Chinese menu
(that just happened to float by) I admit difficulty.

A luminous fringe   O wandering soul
where we find ourselves *inerme*

Captured in "slow-mo"(tion) for all time to come

Lecture on Russian Literature
Delivered inside a Gigantic Banana

for Bill Berkson

Ladies and Gentlemen, Good Day!

I know you must be aware of this most unusual site wherein we find ourselves, but I ask you please focus your attention. My first thought this morning: Gosh, I've got to shave again! (I am sure many of you have had something of a similar experience and thought from time to time, well, possibly excluding you ladies, that is to say, where the act takes a somewhat different turn). Now Peter the Great, the Czar of all the Russias, had an idea,—he actually had a number of good ideas but few in the matter of government,—he had the beards of the Boyars shaved off; this was his first act in bringing about the "modernisation", if you will, of Russia. You will inevitably ask: "What has this to do with Literature?" Well, everything. Its ramifications can be felt this day) with the exceptions of course of Dostoyevsky, Turgenev, and that latter-day rascal, Solzhenitzen, who evidently, resident in the U.S. for a spell, ranted and raved about people on welfare and food stamps and all and called for a new Cold War against Russia, subscribed to Marie Antoinette's dictum, "Let them (the poor and disenfranchised) eat cake!" Well you see where that got *her*. Not a good example for one engaged in Literature, I'd say—either for the Queen or for Mr. Solzhenitzen!

Well, Literature—*Les Lettres*—says,—Russian or otherwise—"Yes, Let them eat cake but also macaroni and baguettes French bread or Russian rye or Greek bread—*yum*, I'm getting hungry already—hot dogs (if they're not vegetarians) and rice and jalapeño peppers and spaghetti and meatballs with heaps of salad greens; washed down with wine, beet, and/or orange juice and brandy; we'll include Napoleons and George Washington cherry tarts in that repast, too." I don't know what Napoleon himself would have thought of those pastries named after him, given his débâcle in Russia, 1812—but we won't worry about that here. Suffice it to say "Literature" personally wishes all a good breakfast—déjeuner and petit déjeuner, as the French say, "lunch" and a good dinner to all: from Russia to Malaysia to China and the Appalachian Mountains. Even to Brooklyn with the ghost of its absent Dodgers!

This is what Literature wishes to say and if any author worth his or her salt is thus engaged this should be his or her credo or wish for all people as well: Let no one go to bed hungry. Let no one suffer the pangs of hunger as once they did in the time of the Czars in Russia. And I am sorry to say this condition of hunger still exists in what passes for the "modern" Russian State brandishing along its betrayed Revolution of 1917, hoisting the flag of McDonald's (with its emblem of the "Big Mac" smack dab in the middle of Red Square.

—*Quel horreur!* Balzac would say.

And yes Balzac isn't Russian nor has he any relation as far as I know to bananas, but Lenin, architect of the Revolution and an author himself (*Empiricism and Dialectical Materialism*) would add to it his own resounding "*Quel Horreur!*"

Well, Ladies and Gentlemen, the time, the time is drawing near: our forty-five minutes are almost "up" as opposed to "down" There was, you see, no apple to fall on the head of a Sir Isaac Newton in Russia so the laws of gravity were unknown there; but I suspect if the housewife of Czar Peter's time held an egg and let it slip from her fingers it *would* land onto the ground with a *splat!*—And the cat would come and lick it up what was on the floor and no doubt would have had in its mind some of the ideas of the laws of gravity even though no Russian thinker had as yet come up with them as yet!
That brings us in the short time we have left to Catherine the Great who wasn't much of a cook and undoubtedly never experimented lifting eggs and letting them purposefully fall to the floor in her boudoir nor speculated upon the philosophical consequences thereof.

Gosh, does anyone smell—*burnt toast?*

Tut Tut, Ladies and Gentlemen! No toasters allowed in our lecture hall, which you can see is a Gigantic (and full ripe) Banana; it could cause some catastrophic *mess!*
Ahem, getting back to Catherine, who wanted to be "Great" like her predecessor, Czar Peter.—although to my knowledge she never shaved off anyone's beard,—she may have, on the other hand, in one of the clandestine exploits in her boudoir,—?—she liked to read books. She even wrote one in Russian which I must say I have not read. But know somehow it had nothing to do with beets or potatoes,—the subject of the book, I mean. I will mention her fanciful correspondence with Voltaire, our French philosophe and perhaps learned a thing or two from him about government?

"Government by the People and FOR the People" ?
Well, that *wasn't* one of them.

Now, Ladies and Gentlemen, Russian Lit., from its inception with the *Song of Igor's Campaign* (ah, the audacity of some who still dare doubt its authenticity! *Tch tch*!) This is all a very rich affair and I invite you all to partake in it—particularly the poetry of *Eugène Onegin* by Pushkin, who was infused like my own ancestors with Ethiopic blood. Now there are others, Russians, who are also named Pushkin—I myself have met at least one—but doubt that these have any Ethiopic blood or for that matter are in any way by bloodline related to the great poet Pushkin, who has been likened to Shakespeare. Yevgenyii, translated as Eugène. French and English, was the husband of the Russian woman I loved and still do *because love* whether in Babylon, Russia, Siberia, Transylvania, or Colchis, *never ends.*

As to that Gigantic Banana that surrounds us I assure you its walls are quite edible as you exit. Bon Appétit!

l' Inconnu (A.D. 2008)
— S.

L' INCONNU (AD 2008)
S.

On Brubeck Way

for Christine Lé

J'habite un voyage de mille ans
   —Aimé Césaire

I don't hear any music coming from the eaves
on my way
I realize I am still
(as they say now) "directionally challenged"
meaning I don't know right from left
Or "East" from "West" except to look
for the sunrise in the East
and its setting in the West

      An inveterate pedestrian
my Mecca resides in a stone or a tree or a
girl's *élan*

Fortunately a landmark in the distance
the R.E. Burns Tower ahead
Which I know to walk "toward"
(unless that is there's a fog
then the tower disappears!)
a saxophone's bobbing
Up the path
I don't hesitate to ask it for directions
    —"Hi!—Hola!"
but it passes me by in a flourish with
no reply

A lovely young woman on Cloud Nine
approaches to stop momentarily she shakes
my hand but doesn't give her phone
number —*Hélas!*

I'm a long way from the *Place de l'Étoile*

For Anne (Waldman)

ET Ainsi Le nom d'Anne c'est partout et je me suis
presqu'ilé d'Elle encore

مُسَافِر (Musafar) *(Pèlerin)*

It has come. I was waiting for it to come. It had been lost.
But now it is "here" The route once again the path the way *(Tariq)*
مِر صود to

resumes
The *page blanc* the blank page neighs beckon me astride

sans frontières I find myself once again voyeuring in the fond of
her illumination   behind the veiled face in the bazaar She glides amongst
skaters in Rockefeller Centre beneath the Angel who hovers above the rink
where I remain but a bystander *anonyme* in the crowd   on the beach I
wander in the summer of her footprints wondering at their direction before
the incoming tide
(I write "One day I wrote her name upon
the strand")
The svelte girl acrobat on the trapeze above the hippodrome who
fascinated my childhood (the height I could never attain)
Her spectral panoplies pervade the spume of the falls at
(the Kaufmann House) Wright's Falling Water

—The infinite number of her images Nefertiti projected of herself—

On the boulevard in Dakar her silhouette displays her grace en route
to the Unnameable (here I yet recall Joe Ceravolo's conversation asking me
if it were "still possible to use the word Beauty in a poem")

Without a country I journey

مُسَافِر

(*Musafar*) in her country between the *Place d'Étoile* in the rose garden at *Malmaison* the silence of the *Cloisters*   St. Mark's Place New York I wear the mask of the Aquila Nera know firsthand the madness of Berlioz her multiple forms in her bring (*l'être*) and becoming absence and *presence* (And here it is the French *Presence* of which I speak) I don't know what to do with my left hand which remains suspended during sleep perimeters "range widely" ukuleles gone to pasture with knights' white horses I procede on my journey that of a Marabout "not knowing where I go or why" my trek leads not to Nepal or Medina but to the expanse of a giant heart that is my horizon

Hommage Perpétual

to Mme. *Frances Lefèbvre (Waldman)*
(Anne's Mother)

Through so many moves I've lost all the letters, the books you sent me, your memories of first meeting Breton during his exile *New York (1944)* (You played Hostesse) but we still embrace you still hold my hand in *Anne's apartment on St. Mark's Place, NYC. Facile* as a girl bats her eyelashes is it possible we can tell by the shape of her fingernails how her toenails will appear?
(One of many questions I never had the opportunity to pose to you, descendent of Diotima's wisdom (in the *Symposium*))
Your richness still enfolds me my Nomad my Fellow Traveller *Toward* The Marvellous
Those moments we spent are now infinite
Sur l'amour d'
Anne how could I not but love *you* who recognized my identity on the instant at our meeting
Finally I've discovered the locale
of *Joë Bousquet's* monumental memoire *Rendez-vous d' un soir d'hiver* (under the imprint of *René Débresse*)
(John Hopkins Library, Special Collections,) I've spoken on the phone to Amy Kimball, (the curator)   left her footprints on the beach at Santa Cruz when she was there as a student her footprints now leave their imprint in my room where the surf can't wash them away
This morning my new book completes *me*
P.S.
I have been *witness* (*Arabic, Shaheed* شاهد): this morning Matt Lauer, host of the TODAY TV Show, presented a bouquet to a young thirteen year-old who fell from her bike and injured her arm (in a cast) I wish I knew her name I would send her a poem. For this is the substance of Poetry.
As I have said before me TV screen is—to quote Peter the Great—"my window to the West" (as he spoke of his St. Petersburg,) Thus
The Marvellous—*Le Merveilleux*—awaits at every corner

We need only leave the "geometry of the intellect" (Bergson) behind and set out on our journey without destination without frontieres
I miss my bottle of Armenian Brandy with which I would *toast each new day

But a daily dose of Vodka and/or American Whiskey suffices for my agoraphobia before I leave the door
I find myself again "in the zone" of the Ineffable

The magic carpet which the Thief of Baghdad flew over his ancient City has just now flown in through my window

NOTE: *toast: as opposed to the proto-imperialist, M. Churchill, who toasted his day with a glass or two of sherry before beginning his writing or a new painting on the canvas

Night of the 28th of December (AD 2008

for Jim Gustaveson, AD 1966–2008

By tomorrow   the socks on the line will dry
they will walk in foreign fields   they will
kick over Aztec heads on coinage even though
I can't see through the night of my idled sunglasses
Paris yes Paris is still "there" along with the click-clicking
high heels of Mlle. Louise Burchille and all the following fol-
de-rah they spout in Paris *Université VI–VII*
Playboy Bunnies you are *ushabtis* of the Pharoah but you cannot
descend as Ishar to search for and find and resurrect Tammuz in the under-
world even though you are my sisters at this hour

socks will freeze   in the *neiges* of Sherbrooke   where

Roséline's breath   leaves its roseates of lace on the
frost of the windowpane of Simard
I never tire of listening to the violin of Anna-Sophie
Mutter play   in J. S. Bach's *Concerto for Violin and Orchestra*
    its tunes play on in my head even when I can't hear
heralding my sanity   everything in the present tense

Rather than in the future imperfect Dante like *Orfeo* had
to discover his love through death in the *Vita* I'm still
manqué of and here Rouault's *Miserèrè* continues its
stare right back at me the plans of mice and men

NOTES:

Tammuz, Babylonian god of wine and poetry, also known as *Dammuzi* in
Akkadian.

Orféo, Orpheus, the primal poet of the world (Greece).

Jim Gustaveson (AD 1966–2008) American Quarterback, Social Activist,
Son-in-Law.

From a Letter to Donald and Luisa Stewart in Rome

Aquela hora de crisis . . . en esto mînuto
—Pablo Neruda, *carta à Miguel Otero en Caracas*
(1949)

Quel est donc ce pays lointain
Qui semble tirer toute sa lumière de ta vie.
—André Breton

There are almond blossoms blowing everywhere

like *a snowstorm* and I'm caught in
the midst   like an ancient Chinese poet

who grabs for his pen   to record

the moment   that even in the writing
                              is gone

As I myself will be one day

But the giant images of *CHE* still stands in *Revolutionary Square*
in Havana   and yes "tent cities" (like the 1930s)
have sprung up here and everywhere
                                        in this land

I cannot duplicate the loaves and fishes effected at Galilee
—*Would that I could!*
                    As I'm seated on the bench
The mall guard cycling up shouts "How do you like the
weather?"
          Ah, it's good   Muy bien
                    مير صود‎ (*Mahbsoud!* (Arabic)]
              C' est bien, alors
The wind turns the pages
of my notebook

229

My socks are still not fully dry O AKKADIAN
emprenta

Yet *I breathe*
I breathe the same air Empedocles breathed upon Mt. Etna!
Air the Queen of Sheba breathed as she traversed
many lands on her journey And we go on
in this air

—ὸλή —The Life of the Universe

continues to flow in us

So a Letter's sent out to Friends like so many others
in *media res* midcourse
and never quite completed
    Here I pause as I had forgotten

about the Simourgh bird who now takes a little bow
in our little skit washing machine across the way
in the laundromat still whirring away
at 12:05 a.m. in the Apartment complex

Past 3 a.m. in Havana now the giant neon image of *CHE*
broods over Revolution Square

I recall in my dreams the lovely young woman
who wrote me a poem

As the Young Alexander Beheld Roxanne . . .
(à prendre plume-en-main)

for Desirée

As the young Alexander beheld Roxanne . . . So I
behold the   woman's beauty of your face

Linear algebra has long passed us by

                              As the halcyon
of the city of Alexandria   positions my stance

eremite of the architecture of   snowflakes   again

    Whilst the investment banker in his Manhattan
    penthouse sits and "smirks"

Though I speak with the tongues of angels and hold
at once in my hand any number of pens

at the ready The road lies still subject and predicate
even though the wind's not yet stirred
     the flag's flutter

Galatéa's statue in her splendid nakedness leans over
in an embrace comes alive in the sculptor's arms

(*Mon ombre*) O my shadow still informs the grass
As evidence this "spectacle of matter" to witness
the azure in her name   By which I come énergumène

disarmed
   in a moment

My residence "here" but a temporary dwelling

It is my *cri*   that goes out
        beyond the nations
  among the stars

My name is Melina Mercouri
    Lenin   Toussaint l' Ouverture
Comrade CHE Guevara

To renew the face of the Earth

I've found this fugitive
alcove along the way
to view the human panorama as it passes by

I Am of the Race of Pushkin

for Karina Alexanyan

. . . .

. . . and D'Anthès's bullet   sweeps on spinning
its trajectory   Awake at night   trying to sleep
It has shot out the eye of the mannequin
                    in Macy's store window
(*Mengistu Lemma and I once watched our reflections together
in that show window between looks at the pretty girls
passing by on San Francisco's Embarcadero Plaza)
        Again the bullet's lodged in the pen between
          my fingers

                        Breaks the heel in two of the beauty's
high-heeled shoes   inseminates
the cloud and poet's word
Throughout all time flows out
    into the landscape below
as in the cities below people hasten with open mouths
trying to catch falling raindrops
tainted cumulus of pollution

Occasionally in some parts of the world it rains roses

However only children can see this now
While the bullet continuing on its path shatters
the mirror of the man lathering up at his morning shave
"*Huh!* What the—"
Goes through the cosmetics case and phials of facial oils
of the display window   whizzing past
the young Business Woman outfitted in her business suit
as she prepares for her day at the office   Dolphins dance
                      with angels
The bust of Nefertiti in the Berlin Museum
remains intact, however, steadfast as ever
The violinist just tuning his strings at the rehearsal

233

of the symphony
A child is asking its mummy for a glass of milk

                                  Someone's
hailing a taxi If you were the Earth you, too, would
be tired of the endless trudge on your surface
of all those army boots slogging in the mud and
on dry land for millenniums   Now substitute *that*

For the poet Pushkin's 67 lines in all dedicated to
                   the beauties of women's feet
    (In *Eugene Onegin*) As out of the fog two figures approach
"a pistol flames" and the trajectory of the shot
finally reaches my heart

NOTE: *Mengistu (Lemma),* poet of Ethiopia, friend. See my poem "With Mengistu Lemma in San Francisco"

"White Noise" on the Information Superhighway

for my daughter, Tatyana Torregian

(*Hiccup!*) I'm   (gasp) D. Gyges   Thus the state of
public opinion bottlenecks If you have a "Ptolomaic view"
of the world the articles   are shoes safety pins rolls of adhesive
tape scissors toothbrushes blank and the brain refuses to remember "Right"
says Witness Mr X "I never forget a face" bells are ringing for White men
Investors getting these "windfalls"

Weird to hear Mickey (Mouse) speaking French

the effort expanded beyond Crusoeville's city limits

Which owns   *Clownumbia The Gem of BLOOD*   went into depression
plus I became known as "the killer" But what's a free
enterprise system after all anyway, *right?*
Never thought I'd "see" the day why manure may show sharp
drop-off in the month (*Dummy!*) But *TRUMP Floor Mr. Dithers*

Tell a Mummy probably wasn't working as hard as ere don't

O here appears strip of human face, saying "Become known
as 'The silent'"

Until we meet again

Katherine Bell of TV Soap "General Hospital"

(Mary Beth Evans)

"... recognized through desire of the Other"

You stand like Briséis of Greek legend with your gown
    setting the fashion for melodramatic tastes
"gang a ghaist" but care not to spin   your lips perhaps
verged toward the *Gare St. Lazare* (of *Monet*)
are yourself the church of melody
sparkling "full of fancy and surprises." I first saw you
in your form amidst the constellations

                    Of the summer sky And here it is
you before me now in the flesh, in my tent. I speak
words to you that span centuries
I am the orphan of the seas
Of Ishmael   the waif of the sands
                It is Nietzsche's *Madman* who
        crashed
his lantern as a legacy we are all
in Exile   while butterflies wing their way

To find their refuge in the secret
Coves of Michoácan

            And the dawn bestows
      its glimmer upon the nib of a minaret in Shiraz

How to prevent such
"unwanted guests" challenging your authenticity
gaining entry to the ball at Windamere?
Nimbus that surrounds the historicity of

the kiss a man places on his wife's forehead upon bringing
her cup of coffee in the morning
And being witness I take myself

To the realm
of the unchartered and unknown
The Lake of Fire (*Feuerbach*) says it's all a reflection
                    of ourselves in our own mirror

                In the matter

Of maintaining
"sanity" in a time of distress

As I find myself within the dark
                            swath of Othello

"Hurry My Verses, Hurry!"

(After Boris Pasternak)
for Felicia de Andréu

I've thought about those piles of
old shopping lists found among my manuscripts
possibly being submitted   as artifacts
                                (witness to my being, *mon être*)

But let these
lines go forth as emissaries

—¡HOLA *Compañera!*—

To find you where you are   somewhere
                        journeying   in midcourse

from "point *A*"   to "point *B*"
I have seen the movie *Roman Holiday* so many times
                                        Audrey Hepburn young
Princess   travelling incognito
I'd account it as one of my manifestos on Poetry

        and Love   *L'Amour Fou*
Of course Plato would again take issue with this   Yet
amazing to watch

                        cinema in reverse on my *VCR.*
à retrouver   In the moment you sit legs crossed   attending
                your early morning lecture   I recover all that I have lost

238

Barbie's Fiftieth Anniversary, 9 March 1959–9 March 2009

Dites-moi qui a volé le secret de la Parole
—L. S. Senghor, *Lettres d' Hivernage*

Here the paparazzo   are already at your door

Which is somewhere
on Cloud Nine   (which place
I cannot enter

Except through the memory
                              of all the women I have ever loved)

I have had the privilege
of undressing you   Or reading to you
from the *Canzoniere* of Dante
as I admit I used to do at age sixteen with Patricia Neuhaus

But here we find ourselves
in the era of Space Travel   (and who could ever believe
this would be a subject for poetry)

You don't have to worry
about "bed mites" I mean when staying in a hotel

Your companion Jasmine the African American girl (quite
chic on the social scene)
confides in you a preference for French men.

At 1:09 a.m.

for Alice Notley

J'écoute au fond de moi le chant
—L. S. Senghor, *Nocturne*

Good Morning *Bonjour*
Paris
No thermometer to measure fever
But my Space Pen can still write upside down
A workday for Paris   trams are a-buzz
Again I hear (through snorrs here)
the click click click of Mlle. Louise Burchille's
high heels en-route to Université de Paris *VIII*

We shan't be long for O the Reader
has a short attention span to be respected
and have not *caritas* I am but
a tinkling cymbal   (Lehar's

Gold and Silver Waltz plays on in my head)
My moustache   itches

"That our eye's focused on earthly things" (Dante)

Between darkness and light
Not enough to open the Gates of Horn

Elle passe 1996

She still passes in my mind and I never knew her name. She passed by young and lithe, bringing her daughter, whom I assumed to be about 6 years old, to school in the morning and then returning with her in the afternoon

I cancelled out in my mind all the opportunities whereby we could possibly meet on those occasions and she would respond to my fatuous introduction awkward as it seemed

But then surrendered to the singular reality of the moment in itself

I watched by the window something of a breeze outside but not much of a breeze as the little girl stopped to pick up a flower or perhaps it was a weed of some kind I couldn't tell for sure as the mom tugged at her daughter's arm urging her to get up so they could be on their way.

Imagined identities for her possibly Ukrainian (immigrant) or French (?), for some reason definitely not American or so I thought I don't know why . . .

The end of June or the beginning of fall? I noted how the shrub in front of the house moved ever so slightly when brushed by the wind Inevitably then I thought of Monet patiently waiting throughout all the hours of the day to capture the play of light and shadow on the Cathedral of Chartes each with its variation.

I was alone in the house. The landlady who was mad was away for the day.

About 1 p.m. she was there again across the street taking her child back home. (In the morning they headed in the left direction; in the afternoon they headed right) As she passed at that moment again I noted how the breeze caught a strand of her blonde hair.

Variations on a Rococo Theme

I don't know why but I don't think I've ever listened so closely to Tchaikovsky's *Variations on a Rococo Theme* as I have today. In it are listening the hapless fifty million who perished in those five years of what was called "The Great Patriotic War" (I think particularly of Leningrad) . . . Yet another *nuit blanche* for me. The turgid heat of the day engulfing the room throughout the night. 5:10 a.m. I go to the mirror to see whose face it is that appears in it today. Are you somewhere perhaps deciding at this moment whether to wear stockings or not with your high-heeled shoes as you prepare for your work day? Headlines in the discarded newspaper announce "DREAM BIG"

I used to pour over the *Letters* of Spinoza hoping to find some basic principle by which to live I came away with only the dictum *sub species aeternitatis* I procrastinate in emptying the cat's litter tray but I know I must attend to it soon today I say you can even find poetry there if you look hard enough

"Are those Pernods coming yet?" asks Maigret.

"In a jiffy," says the waiter.

I hate Pernod. (*Me*)

I sit here like a Menhir.

NOTES:

* *sub species aeternitatis,* Latin, under the aspect of eternity.

* *Maigret*: traduction, "*La Guinguette a deux sous*", Simenon.

Pour Saluer Encore René Magritte

(Musé René Magritte, Bruxellles en hommage

À Mme. Virgine Devilles

Mon salut comme un aile claire? Pour te dire ceci
—Léopold Sédar Senghor, *Lettres d' hivernage*

No doubt the choo-chooing locomotive's still exiting
from the mantle of the fireplace   I don't know why
I'm exhausted already just thinking about it
A young *musiciènne* clarinet player's about to embark
for further study in Tennessee of all places I happened
to run into her yesterday (*Mlle.* Angelique) by chance she was wearing
sandals for the first time
Now you know my secret (which could be on the threshold of the ineffable)
It's what happens these days when I lose or misplace things
Which happens more often than not I'm afraid
I don't have Ogotummeli's Dogon cosmology committed to memory

That balcony in Verona where Romeo and Juliette once stood now they're
charging money for lovers to stand there an indication
of "where the world is going" But I don't worry
I have my own world
not quite like Leibnitz's monadology but comparable

Its sunset and sunrise meet in a woman's eyes as she pauses to speak
the name of René Magritte

Personne

for Mme. Devillez

Empty notebook 9 o'clock (p.m.). Nothing to write. But billions of (English) words are waiting. Waiting to be called up, invoked, evoked. Oh Voco vocare. 6th of June: Omaha Beach (1944) bodies in a sea of blood floating off the shores of Normandy. Haven't heard a word on "D-Day" today. The usual droll ceremonies "For God-King and Country" . . . Well "God" hasn't anything to do with war hysteria and lies to get young men to die, Germans—*boche*— Frenchmen, Americans, British . . . that blunderbus prof. of phil*OSO-PHY* in *All Quiet on the Western Front* (Erich Maria Remarque)—he's still the prototype prepping kids for cannon fodder; faithful servant of the Establishment where Security must be maintained at all times, at all costs ("Post-9/11 Nightmare" hasn't changed the color of *lies*) Feed the War Machine. Mint the medals for valour. Here the array of severed legs severed arms severed heads all parading up the avenue. *Dies Irae* do a dance, the *Totentanz* of Death.
Voici: There, the words are *written*.
Would that they had been a love song.

To Mme. Devillez, *Bruxelles*:
Instead of writing "personnel" on the envelope of the letter I sent you I mistakenly wrote "personne" instead. Only now—since the letter was posted and on its way in the mail—did I realize and feel startled by this faux-pas. Then I recognized it was a kind of "Surrealist act" in itself, as poetry disclosed itself out of this apparent error. The *personne*, No one, sent the letter to you. The *personne*. Anyone who might receive it. The *personne* is going to *personne*. No one to No one. One to one. I just left out the "l" at the end of the word. I don't know what the postal clerks seeing this written on the envelope might think. Perhaps they had a good laugh . . . Yet it is from a *personne*, one obviated by poetry. Il parlera "personne (l)"
I am reminded of the days when I used to stamp AVEUGLE on all my letters. Perhaps now I should inscribe "personne" on all outgoing post instead?

This calls for a Dagwood sandwich.

> "Le deversité, sur terre, des idomes,
> empêche *personne* de proférer les mots qui,
> sinon se trouversaient, par une frappe
> unique, elle-même matériellement la verité."
> —Mallarmé
> *Langage Et Mystère*

My Left Arm's Asleep

for Andrei Codrescu

My left arm's asleep   Although
    I'm not in a hotel
But there are memories
of hotels in my left arm   I have just
come upon a snippet of my own
"If we love someone we free them"
    (I've not been very good in adhering to this
                         my own)
oracular pronouncement / If this were Paris
it wouldn't be any better
Shadows
keep passing by my door (near 5 p.m.)
Here's the "efflux of the soul" again
Can all of life be encapsulated in some 8 lines (?)
    ¡Sigue La Lucha!
                 Just in time to view on TV the price
           of gold shilly-shally on the market
Announced by Suzanne Pratt's lovely face
(*Here the African Prince's deep obéissance*)
It is you talking just as much as myself

Où la Vrai Vie, or, the "Real" Surreal Life

"I went up to the mountain to look for myself.
I was not there."
—Chinese poem

"*Notarysojack!*"
—Barney Stover Comics

"or a room lost within its exact locality"
—Andrew Joron, *Sound Mirror*

I have been asked why it is I still identify myself as a "(French) Surrealist."

"French" I claim not by nationality but by vision, as I see the world, as it were, translated into the French language, which I consider to be the most superior of all modern languages, given that the greatest poetry—and poets of our time—has come down to us in that language (I don't give a fig for the opinions of the Academy of the French Language, whether it is pure or "impure", marred by foreign elements, Americanisms, etc. And I am more delighted to hear Africans speak French than I am listening to native Parisian speakers. And I say, *Bravo!* à les Quebec-oises!) I like it when I come upon the word Harlem in French.)

On my bookshelves are the works of Paul Éluard, St. John Perse, a lovely inscribed edition of his *Oeuvre Poétique* by my friend, Léopold Sédar Senghor; and the magnaminity of the poems of my friend, Jean Paul Guibbert, *La Chair Du Monde*, wherein the introduction states that "*la Beauté*—source de toute souffrance et de tout *émerveillement*". I stand by these words in any language.

I know French was one of the languages my forebearers spoke not necessarily by choice but by conquest, being a part of the once-imperial France and its colonies.
Each year Aimé Césaire and I celebrate the same birthday, 25th of June, which, it happens, is also the birthday of "*Surrealisme*", so-proclaimed by the magnificent Apollinaire in Paris, 1917, during the author's introduction to his Surrealist poem–play, *Les Mamelles De Tiresias*.

In the meantime inside me, all my ancestors continue to converse in their respective languages: Arabs, Greeks, Armenians, Assyrians, ETHIOPIANS—

my African counterpart!—the sounds and textures of *Ge'ez*, Carthaginian, Byzantine-Greek, as well as the Greek of Homer's time, the Armenian of Cappadocia, Phoenician of Mt. Lebanon (*Liban*) Coptic of Egyptian traders, Arabic of the *Moors of medieval Sicily* and of Al-Andalus, AKKADIAN, and Assyrian of the Fertile Crescent . . .

Albanians, intoning their hymns to Giorgis Castriotis, or Scanderbeg, in their flight from Ottoman domination in the Balkan peninsula . . . Ah, I have forgotten Persian. I am sure in this tide of immigrants, there were Persian speakers in there too,—how else would I recognize the *"Tavern of Ruin"* of Hafiz to be also my own dwelling?

Ah, but my ancestors, I cannot respond to your cries replicating them in your own language even as you continue to converse in my blood, *I continue to speak and write in an adopted language, English*, even as James Joyce, that polyglot poet, once declared he, too, wrote in an adopted tongue, that of the English Colonists who had overtaken his own native Irish soil (Here recall the horror of the miscreant Cromwell and the slaughter of Drougheda! and the tyranny that followed); yet, the poet triumphed in exile to re-create the English language. re-inventing it for himself.

I "see" the world as a Surrealist.
Yet when I say this it is without the rather dogmatic views of a Mentor, founder, of the Surrealist Adventure, André Breton.

For me the created world continues to reveal its marvels spontaneously, through amblings, through unexpected encounters, through dreams . . . Here I have "found objects" before me (*objets trouvées*); here the furtive gaze of a beautiful woman as she passes me on the street becomes the lines of a new poem . . . here with me still are the words of Whitman, which I first discovered when I was but a teenager, found in the *Leaves of Grass* of the great American Mentor

"I find letters from God in the street and each one is signed with God's name" . . .. Flying Saucers? No, I don't believe I have ever encountered any. But we don't need to go to the South Seas like Gauguin to find the *Marvelous*, as it waits behind every corner. It was only a few days ago this experience occurred to me. I knew that Picasso in his early days would traverse the streets of Paris searching through trash to create his found objects of art. Well the day before yesterday, I found a Picasso in the trash! It was a large portrait of *Marie-Thérèse Walter*, which undoubtedly some dunce had discarded with the exclamation, "*Ick*, such an ugly painting, who needs it!"

—and so the endlessness of poetry goes on! A poetry that transcends the English and the French Language. (And yes, I write "in French" as well with that same spirit that lead Rimbaud to declare "J'*est* un Autre") . . . it is something *beyond, Au-de-là*

And I must say I discover discarded clothes hangers from someone's wardrobe in the trash as well. Who knows how many hangers one might need in one's closet . . . No, this poetry goes quite beyond the American idea of "poetry", beyond "French," even. *Sur-réalité. Mon Altérite.* Apollinaire's words introduced the word, *surréalisme* to the French and then the English language, introduced therein by my friend, David Gascoyne, English Surrealist poet extraordinaire, in 1934, in his *Short Survey of Surrealism.*

Any competent library will give the reader all the information he or she will need to know *about* Surrealism, French or otherwise. I find such recounting enervating. One will learn that Surrealism in France, after its heyday in the 1920s, became somewhat stultified, codified with what was correct and incorrect, what was Surrealist or not, and who was read out of the Surrealist Group for overstepping the lines into "literature" or taking "art" seriously, (or, like David Gascoyne becoming a Catholic convert through his study of the great mystics who themselves had enthralled the Surrealists, ironically enough. Raymond Lully, Meister Eckhart, Ruysbroeck, to name a few . . .) this grand new spirit congealed into stratification, taking itself too seriously . . . Yet Breton remains for me most luminous in his *being*, despite his inclination toward oligarchy as Spokesman for the French Surrealist Group.

It is now 9:31, and I grow weary of exegesis.

The Surrealist Adventure remains unconfined in the human spirit.
There's no one any longer to march in step with or out of step with the dictates of the commander of the Surrealist faithful.

There is only **I.* That I that perceives the world and through whom poetry whatever that is continues to emanate. *Vers*) Toward (*The Marvellous*

Yet that *I* is in community with Others. Which equals *Revolution.* The *Permanent Revolution* as espoused by Breton, Trotsky, and Diego Rivera, with the artist free to follow where his or her muse takes him or her. I still appreciate the One and the Many, the Pythagorean view of the world. I should also say typing, these days, makes me somewhat seasick and I look forward to complete my seafaring as Sinbad and find harbour.

NOTE: *I, *Le Moi*, non l'état De! maintenant De Ce qui constitue l'individualité. That is, not that "I", that Self, that proclaims itself "The State" but that Self that constitutes individual being.

Musique de le Temple du Gloire

Merci por mon mouchoir mon petit déjeuner (*J' ai oublié*) Chere Mademoiselle Ne trouvez pas qu'un pareil souvenir un cadre ovale garni de cordes tendues—C' est ne C' est pas pour marcher sur la neige? Où non parce qu'ici c'est l'été encore Il éclora Où est-elle? Elle ne connaîtrait pas mon viasge et je
ne reconnaîtrait pas
le son de sa voix Possible un *klaxon* qu'est le plus ancien

souvenir de mon coeur? *D'alors* la plage la plage dans la maison je n'ai retrouvé (*Où va notre jeunesse!*)
Et vous, vous jouait avec les Ruines de Babylon le melodrame de nos vies en ce pays
Voici j'ai sauvé la reine de l'Angleterre!
Je n'y ai pas pensé seulement un instant
Je tomberai peut-être dans tes bras
la pomme d'or décernée a Vénus par Vénus (le prémier non La Cité de parasitaires d' aujourd'hui!) le fils de Priam et quit fut le ravisseur d'Hélène un voile de nuages cherchant le verrre un veille église est dans l'*intérieure*
Je ne sais pas pourquoi nous avons arrêter ici Le dépôt de nos souvenirs et nous rendent un charmant fantôme d'elles Le berceau du "Langage" même le lyre-du-laitier ô honte je me suis assis ici tout-a-fait nue et je songe de Galatée la sculpture vivante devant moi ici
(Il était que je n'ai jamais compris L'Ordonnance du Langage et son âtre Les sombres itineraires du sort ne peuvent être étudiés sans un profond serrement de coeur

Music of the Temple of Glory

Thank you for my handkerchief my breakfast (I forgot)
Dear Miss Don't you think that such a memory an oval frame garnished with
stretched cords—It is Isn't it to walk on snow? Or not because here it is still
Summer It will bloom Where is she? She would not know my face and I
would not recognize the sound of her voice Possibly a *taxi horn* what is the
farthest memory of my heart? From then the beach the beach in the house I
did not find again (Where is our youth going!)
And you, for you playing with the Ruins of Babylon the melodrama of our
lives in the country
Here I have saved the queen of England!
I did not think of it as a single moment
Maybe I will fall in your arms
The golden apple awarded to Venus by Paris (the first not The City of
parasites today!) the son of Priam and who was the kidnapper of Hélène a
veil of cloud searching for the glass an old church is within the *interior*

I do not know why we stopped here The depository of our memories
And give us back a charming ghost of them The cradle of "Language" itself
the Lyre of the milkman
O shame I sat down here completely naked and I dream of Galatea the living
sculpture alive in front of me here
(It was that I never understood *The Ordinance* of Language and its hearth
The dark itineraries of fate cannot be studied without a deep heaviness of
heart

NOTES:

* English Translation from the original French of the poet by *Mme.* Hélène
Laroche-Davis

klaxon, Avertisseur d'auto. Car horn, also taxi horn.

Pour Eleni Sikelianos

prendrai un logique entier pour vous et pour moi ma Chère *j'ai mille choses
diverse* Quel autre pays où l'on exerce la marchandîse chacun y est tellement
plaisirs des les fables les jours parmi la confusion
Mais je les comprends comme eternelles et
autant de liberté et de   immauables
                          repos   Et si vous
demande où je suis je vous prie de dire que je
n'en êtes pas certain parce que j'étais en
resolution   de passer en *l'aurore boréale* que
      se recontrent en vos forêts Au lieu qu'en

        cette grand ville de la raison les trahisons et toutes les curiosités que
peuvent être bananes demeuré plus de reste de l'innocence de nos chansettes
encore *Quel pays où l' on puisse* ces etincelles ma vie c' est à dire sans être
jamais vu de personne je préferer ce préfet de la rivage je vous dire qu je
n'eusse su trouver les fondaments de (la) les rêveries que celui de quelque
      ruisseau . . . les longues chaînes de la raison pour les déduire les une des
autres *Qui?* vous perdre votre clé cependent de la Muse je fais mes apéritifs si
vous plaît ne fantômes ne carrotes
      Et vous? Étes—vous né a New York Non non monsieur je suis né à Londres
voici les allumettes cher monsieur j'ai tout c' q'il me faut maintenant Il vous
faut un plus grand girafe pour ma part *et* Quelle est la grandeur de cette
chambre continue *où* discontinue chacun suivant le reconnaissance de
parachutistes   lumineuses aprés un   .
                          égarement de mille âns. Ainsi
j' aime ce femme

For Eleni Sikelianos

will take a whole logic for you and for me
I have a thousand various things What other country where one exercises
merchandise everyone is there so much
pleasures of the fables days among confusion
But I understand them as eternal and
as much freedom and   unchangeable
                              repose   And if you
ask where I am I beg you to say that I am not certain because I was
in resolution   to pass into the aurora borealis which
are found in your forests   Instead in this big city of reason treasons and
all curiosities that can be bananas
remained more leftover of the innocence of our
little songs still Which country where one can these
sparks my life that is to say without ever being
seen by anyone I prefer this prefect of the
shore I tell you that I would not have known how to find
the foundations of the reveries than the one of some
creek . . . the long chains of reason to deduct one from the others Who?
you lose you key however of the Muse I make
my appetizers if you please no ghosts no carrots
And you? Were you born in New York No no
Sir I was born in London here are the
Matches dear sir I have all I need now You need a taller
Giraffe for me and what is the size of
this bedroom continue or discontinue each
according the recognition of luminous parachutists
after wandering for a thousand years. Thus
I love this woman

—English Translation from the original French of the poet by *Mme.*
Hélène Laroche-Davis

Gare de l'Est

Gare d' (À Mme. Amy Kimball)

C'est) la Gare d'   une moment   très chère Voix
de ma dame sur le teléphone ainsi Mon Vendome ma vent
                              Ma Rome
resurgit   mon expatriation   Adieu   mon anglais mon manquée
    carnaval de mon peau charges d'affaires
                                        d'Afrique
ne pas plus de café (? L'heure sonnera dans le bureau
de Mme. Maxine Groffsky (en N.Y.C) Encore Bonjour
                              maquignonesse du coeur
À savoir Sa-Voix Ma Papaguénette
En ce manière je me fait maniaque d'alors
                              *chaman des tous chemins
En elle   je chante tout le monde
Je me suis mansardé d'abord   *En elle* Le Trois Coups le quartet
sonné   quel route *Orfèvrié*   mon fèvre mon infirmier-
    esse ici mon oeuf est froid déjà en avant de
sa sourire joyeux et sans ironie   Le bahut s'arrête
toujours à la même place là quand le dieu de la guerre
La foule l'on timbalais "Ah, Jerry! Jerry!" la douche s'arrête
Soudain les receptions   avaient cessé

Fr., *chaman - Shaman, (anglais

Gare de L'est (East Station)

Station d' (To Ms. Amy Kimball

This is the Station of a moment dearest Voice
Of my lady on the telephone My Vendome my wind
                                    My Rome
Reappears my expatriation   Good-bye my English my missed
Carnival of my skin chargés d'affaires

                                        Of Africa
No no more coffee (? The hour will strike in the office
of Mrs. Maxine Groffsky (in NYC) Again Hello
                        lady horsetrader of the heart
That is to say Her-Voice   My papaguénette
In this way I become manacle of that time
                *shaman of all paths

In her   I sing the world
I garreted myself first In her opening *Curtain-Call the quartet
Rang   which way   jeweler my brother my nurse
  here my egg is already cold before
her joyous smile without irony The bus always stops
at the same place there   when the god of war
The crowd carted around "Ah, Jerry! Jerry! "the shower stops
Suddenly receptions   had stopped

English translation from the original French of the poet by Mme. Hélène
Laroche-Davis

NOTES:

*shaman, French *chaman*

Les Trois Coups, signal in French theatres for raising the curtain.

NOTE: to GARE DE L'EST Ms) *Maxine Groffsky*, one of former editors of *Art
and Literature* (Isère, France) and the *Paris Review* (Paris and New York),
1960s; *maquinignonesse*, French, feminine, horse tamer; *Papaguénette*,
feminine counterpart of Papagueno in Mozart's *Die Zauberflöte, (The Magic
Flute); Chaman*, French, *Shaman; Les Trois Coups,* signal in French theatres
for curtain to go up; *Orfèvrié*, French, goldsmith, act of goldsmithing.

A Significant Entry in the Author's Journal

I am too tired to write tonight.
I'll write tomorrow.

El Voici déja Aujourd'hui Je l'écris:
"*Demain*"

—S. T.
16. *viii.* AD 2009

*And here it is: I've written "Tomorrow" (!))
—S. T.

The Gordian Knot Untied

Gordios, roi de la Phrygie, lié un noeud très compliqué. Un oracle promettait l'empire d'Asia à celui qui réussirait à le défaire. *Alexandre le Grand le trancha d'un coup d'epée.*

Gordios, king of Phrygia, tied a very complex knot. An oracle predicted the empire of Asia would fall to him who successfully untied the knot. Alexander the Great cut it in two with a blow of his sword.

Stop right there where you are
And ask yourself if it's worth conducting a series
of lectures and entertainments occasioning
the pelf of a continent (*l'Asie il n'avait pas changé*)

Not cancelling before the "free trial period"
"Let's keep going", said Penny
Change of scenery in the shortest
amount of time
Ah, bellwether of my torpor!

Italians don't add oil when boiling their pasta

       the central sulcus
or "fissure of Rolando"

As I conceive of myself   as being in space
and consequently have
an "outside" view of myself
I find myself   dreaming of very far-off days
Bucephalus plummage
               From where
As I stand now
"new" will be "old" And I will again have "been"

Nuit d' Éclosion

Dans la Nuit d' Éclosion

Oui, dans cette miroir de mes mots écrivait de mon "semblable mon frère
"je me regarde le vrai visage de moi-même (En face de la jeune-fille qui
encore traverse-le-nage dans le mirage du désert dans mon oreille)

ô mots   ô blessures   qui frappe une marteau de rayon-de-lune
sur ma campagne
Le reveille roulett-russe de 3e heures au matin

D'ailleurs ceci Londres est a flot dans ses propres larmes

Blooming Night

The Night in Bloom.

Yes, in this mirror of my words wrote of "my kin, my brother"
I look at the true face of myself
(In front of   the young girl who crosses the—swim in the mirage of the
desert of my ear)

O words   o wounds   which strike a hammer of moonbeam on my
countryside
The wake up Russian roulette of the third hour in the morning

Besides this London is afloat in its own tears

English translation from the original French of the poet by Mme. Hélène
Laroche-Davis

"AINSI
J'ENTENDS L'AUTRE
QUI BRÛLE DANS
UNE RÉGIN PROSPÈRE"

"AND SO . . ..
I HEAR THE OTHER'S
LONGING IN A PROSPEROUS REGION"

For Mme. Hélène Laroche-Davis:
As One Poem Becomes the Key to Another

D'un cours orageux,/ Roule, plein
de gravier, *sur un terrain sans but*

So I continue to roam   in my *Wanderlehrer* mode
the realm of your name   and its origins
through one who was blind (*Aveugle*)
as parapets of Ilion gave evidence
        but a wraith in Helen's form held captive there
Her beauty comes again to reside in the shadows

Of my heraclitean bed   (announced by
        ephors of the Armenian script of Meshdots
and fanfares of Ethiopic *Ge'ez*

I remove my watch from my wrist
as Jean Valjean removes shackles from his limbs

A few pennies scattered on the floor I pace over them

On my rounds of Canossa in this room

Her grace even as rising from sleep she stands barefoot

        before the aperture of the refrigerator door
a lit transparence to her negligee in the dark of the kitchen
                        at 3 a.m.

A long way from Combray
I eschew news   of the orbiting astronaut's return to Earth
In preference to
the empyrean of your own woman's mind
its smaragdine knowledge   by which I am uplifted
to set my course in the minutiae of everyday

To whom I transmit strains of the *Africa Suite* of Saint-Saëns

261

At the Taj Mahal   a perpetual
noon but the bench upon which the young princess sat
is vacant now

I've never been to *Le Procope*

                  Where the uvular "r" dances like a star
In the chancellery of the future
having found my way here
in this eleatic locus to redisover

Eternal youth in Hélène's desmesne

NOTES:

Ge'ez: Ancient language of Ethiopia, now extinct, still used as liturgical language of the Ethiopian Orthodox Church.

Combray: France, associated with Proust's early years where his family resided.

At the Taj Mahal: reference
                is to Princess Diana (1961–1996) Princess of Wales, who visited the Taj Mahal in the early 1990s.

Le Procope: famous French restaurant, Paris, founded 1686.

"FINALEMENT! Jᴇ sᴜɪs ᴀʀʀɪᴠᴇ́ ʟᴀ̀ J'ᴀᴅᴏʀᴇ ᴄᴇᴛᴛᴇ ʟɪᴠʀᴇ!"
"(Tʀᴀɴsʟᴀᴛɪᴏɴ: "Aʜ, ꜰɪɴᴀʟʟʏ ɢᴏᴛ ᴛʜᴇʀᴇ! I ʟᴏᴠᴇ ᴛʜɪs ʙᴏᴏᴋ!)" S. T., Aᴘʀɪʟ, ᴀᴅ 2012]

ON THE PLANET WITHOUT VISA

Biographe of the Poet, Sotère Torregian

Sotère Torregian traces his varied ancestry to the Aghlabid Moors of the island of Sicily in the Mediterranean. As with his friend, the French Surrealist poet, Senghor, Torregian calls himself "métisse," that is, a person of colour with other strains, including Ethiopic, Arabic, Greek, Armenian (Byzantine) and central Asian admixture in his ancestry, which colours, so to speak, the poet's cultural perspective). Proud of his affiliation with the French Surrealists, that tendency is reflected in his writing, with French phrases along with Arabic, Spanish, and Italian at times intermingled in the text of the poem.

Torregian attended Rutgers University (philosophy and classics), leaving there to join with the New York School of Poets and Artists (1962–1967). He taught at the Free University of New York until 1967, when with his first wife, Kathleen, he relocated to the West Coast to take residence in California where he has remained to this date. In 1968 he joined with Dr. St. Clair Drake to be his assistant in the newly formed African American Studies Program at Stanford University. There Torregian developed and taught his own lecture series, a Marxist critique of African and third-world philosophy. As one of the leaders of the antiwar movement, Torregian was dismissed from his post along with others in 1975, after which—his marriage having dissolved—as a single parent he worked as a librarian-assistant, a visiting lecturer to various universities, wrote, and gave readings from his books.

Among his awards, the poet was designated "Author of the Year" in 1976 by Gotham Book Market, New York, on publication of his book *The Age of Gold Poems, 1968–1970* by Kulchur Press, New York. He was also recipient of the Kulchur Foundation's Frank O'Hara Award for Poetry.

There are to date some fifteen books of the poet's work extant, the latest being *On the Planet without Visa*. Other notable publications include *The Golden Palomino Bites the Clock* (Angelhair, 1966), *The Wounded Mattress* (Oyez, 1968), *City of Light* (Paris and San Francisco, 1971), *Amtrak Trek* (Telephone Books, 1979), and *"I Must Go" (She Said) "Because My Pizza's Cold": The Selected Works 1957–1999* (Skanky Possum Press, 2002).

The poet currently resides in the city of Stockton, California, with a cat named "Gigi."

Biographe of the Translator, Mme. Hélène Laroche-Davis

Madame Hélène Laroche-Davis is an author, scholar and professor of French language and literature, author of the classic, *Robert Desnos, Une Voix, Un Chant, Un Cri* (Robert Desnos, a voice, a song, a cry) (Paris: Roblot, 1981), a commentary and biography of the great French Surrealist poet, now used in many university French literature classes. Born and raised in Lyon, France, Dr. Laroche-Davis taught in the French department at Stanford (1966–1973). A connoisseur of French cinema, she founded the French Ciné-Club, Palo Alto, California. She is currently professor of French and cinematic studies at Notre Dame de Naumur University, where she also directs the foreign language department. Professor Dr. Laroche-Davis enjoys many distinguished honors for her scholarship and writing, among which have been a fellowship at the University of Monpellier, France, *Palmes Academiques* from the French government, and the 2008 George Keller Teaching Excellence Award at Notre Dame de Namur University. *Professor Hélène Laroche-Davis and the author, poet S. T., have enjoyed a friendship from 1968*, a friendship that has inspired the poet with many poems and new revelations of the Marvellous.

Coffee House Press

MISSION

The mission of Coffee House Press is to publish exciting, vital, and enduring authors of our time; to delight and inspire readers; to contribute to the cultural life of our community; and to enrich our literary heritage. By building on the best traditions of publishing and the book arts, we produce books that celebrate imagination, innovation in the craft of writing, and the many authentic voices of the American experience.

VISION

LITERATURE. We will promote literature as a vital art form, helping to redefine its role in contemporary life. We will publish authors whose groundbreaking work helps shape the direction of 21st-century literature.

WRITERS. We will foster the careers of our writers by making long-term commitments to their work, allowing them to take risks in form and content.

READERS. Readers of books we publish will experience new perspectives and an expanding intellectual landscape.

PUBLISHING. We will be leaders in developing a sustainable 21st-century model of independent literary publishing, pushing the boundaries of content, form, editing, audience development, and book technologies.

VALUES

Innovation and excellence in all activities
Diversity of people, ideas, and products
Advancing literary knowledge
Community through embracing many cultures
Ethical and highly professional management and governance practices

Funders

Coffee House Press is an independent nonprofit literary publisher. Our books are made possible through the generous support of grants and gifts from many foundations, corporate giving programs, state and federal support, and through donations from individuals who believe in the transformational power of literature. Coffee House Press receives major operating support from the Bush Foundation, the Jerome Foundation, the McKnight Foundation, from Target, and in part by a grant provided by the Minnesota State Arts Board through an appropriation by the Minnesota State Legislature from the state's general fund and its arts and cultural heritage fund with money from the vote of the people of Minnesota on November 4, 2008. Support for this title was received from the National Endowment for the Arts, a federal agency. Coffee House also receives support from: several anonymous donors; Elmer L. and Eleanor J. Andersen Foundation; Suzanne Allen; Around Town Literary Media Guides; Patricia Beithon; Bill Berkson; the James L. and Nancy J. Bildner Foundation; the E. Thomas Binger and Rebecca Rand Fund of the Minneapolis Foundation; the Patrick and Aimee Butler Family Foundation; Ruth and Bruce Dayton; Dorsey & Whitney, LLP; Mary Ebert and Paul Stembler; Fredrikson & Byron, P.A.; Sally French; Jennifer Haugh; Anselm Hollo and Jane Dalrymple-Hollo; Jeffrey Hom; Carl and Heidi Horsch; Stephen and Isabel Keating; the Kenneth Koch Literary Estate; the Lenfestey Family Foundation; Ethan J. Litman; Carol and Aaron Mack; Mary McDermid; Sjur Midness and Briar Andresen; the Rehael Fund of the Minneapolis Foundation; Schwegman, Lundberg & Woessner, P.A.; John Sjoberg; Kiki Smith; Jeffrey Sugerman; Patricia Tilton; the Archie D. & Bertha H. Walker Foundation; Stu Wilson and Mel Barker; the Woessner Freeman Family Foundation; Margaret and Angus Wurtele; and many other generous individual donors.

ART WORKS.
arts.gov

MINNESOTA
STATE ARTS BOARD

TARGET.

To you and our many readers across the country,
we send our thanks for your continuing support.

Good books are brewing at coffeehousepress.org

COLOPHON

On the Planet without Visa was designed at Coffee House Press,
in the historic Grain Belt Brewery's Bottling House near downtown Minneapolis.
The text is set in Garamond with Bell Gothic Light for display.